"The fruit of righteousness : tree of life : a wins souls is : Proverbs 11:5 -

Blessings
Connie Gambier :)

INTER GALACTIC DANCING

GIFT TO A WEARY WORLD: 'INSPIRATIONS AND REFLECTIONS'

BY CONNIE GAMBRIEL

Xulon
PRESS

TABLE OF CONTENTS

Endorsements

As a pastor, you periodically meet a person whose life is a demonstration of the love of God. Connie is truly such a person. As I read her devotional writings, I marvelled at the Lord's faithfulness to her and her faithfulness to the Lord. In her life, she has walked out the wisdom and encouragement that she received from the Lord while sitting at His feet over many years.

This book is filled with words of wisdom and strength written by a woman who is deeply in love with Him. She has journeyed with her hand in the hand of the Lord. He has brought her through the different seasons of her life, where she did not die in the wilderness, but came out stronger, richer, wiser and yet completely leaning upon her beloved.

Her desire has been to be a bridge between Israel and Canada and prayer for both nations is woven through her writings. God has placed in the hands of Connie the "pen of a ready writer" and within this book are both deep spiritual truths and simple answers to daily problems that come along in life. This is a gold mine filled with insight on how to walk in the difficult seasons of life and to trust the answers that are given by the Holy Spirit.

Our interns here in our School of Destiny have had the privilege of sitting under the teachings of this anointed woman of God. Connie is a retired teacher who has used her retirement to teach and inspire many to love the Lord, to win souls and to love Israel. Our interns have been privileged to receive most of these nuggets and have had strength, endurance, overcoming power and wisdom built into them.

May you be strengthened and encouraged in your daily walk as you glean from all that the Lord has given to her and may her passion for Jesus and for souls be imparted into your life through these writings.

Dr. Gertruda Armaly
Senior Pastor of Antioch Christian Ministries
Essex Ontario, Canada

As I read through Connie's manuscript I could hear her speaking to the students she has taught, the strangers encountered on busy streets and family who have been nurtured with her wonderful collection of experiences.

One of these experiences is reflected in the section; "What is God's book report about my life?" It is a question only to be answered from heaven's perspective.

After my name I see numbers—so many in all
They're the souls that have answered Your heavenly call.

I was fortunate or should, I say blessed to have been one of those numbers that answered heaven's call as Connie presented the gospel to me many years ago.

The format lends itself to devotional study as Connie has a knack for 'squirreling away' pieces of memorabilia which become a mosaic of wisdom teachings. This one borrowed from Bill Wilson…"*It's not so much what you accomplish in life, but what you set in motion*" testifies to her approach to evangelism and spreading the Good News. I can't think of anyone who has set more people in motion towards their destiny.

The pages are filled with speaking God's faith over your situation. Her life and vocabulary dwell on His promises, drawing always from the character of God and not on the temporary bumps in the road we all encounter.

This is not a finished work by any means. Connie daily adds to this collection of encounters and musings viewing life around her with a 'generous eye'. This collection of God insights and God encounters should stir every reader to consider their own journal as a testimony to the faithfulness of God.

Claude Page DDS
Antioch Christian Ministries
Essex Ontario, Canada

Acknowledgments

Thank You Holy Spirit for leading me and guiding me. Special thanks to you, Pastor Gertruda Armaly! Your generous words of kindness in your Endoresement were an encouragement to me. You are not only my pastor, but also my long-time, faithful friend.

Thank you also, Claude Page for your Endorsement. You are one of my godly pastors, my dentist, and my former high school student. Your words are a blessing to me!

To Mary Showell, my dear loyal friend of many years, thank you for the editing that you did.

To Margaret Nikita, God bless you for your countless hours of helping me make modifications Your dedication has assisted me tremendously.

Thank you, dear loving sister Theresa. You provided the picture for the back cover from your inexhaustible collection of pictures through http://www.sendoutcards.com/70915

Thank you, Daniel Caza, for the beautiful cover of my book. Your design is amazing! See: www.creativedeepend.com

To Xulon Press, God bless you for helping me make this book become a reality.

INTRODUCTION

In January of 1995, I began a new journal entitled, "Inspirations and Reflections."

Each entry was dated until the middle of 2013. My intent was twofold: to enable me to remember some of the insights that I was receiving; to be mindful of the wonderful revelations from the Holy Spirit! I didn't want to forget any of these precious nuggets and I remembered what someone once said, "Paper doesn't forget". Some years there were a few entries and other years there were many. At no time did I ever sense that this might become a book. This wasn't even on the periphery of my mind.

During the Christmas holidays I would make it my habit to reread what I had written during the past year. However, during Christmas 2012 I reread the whole journal and was refreshed and encouraged by it. I knew the Holy Spirit had spoken through me: there was this sense that the words were so refreshing because they came to me from God — they were not my own. Then, I considered the fact that possibly others who read these entries might likewise be inspired and refreshed. It was at that moment, this book was born!

To that end I would say, "Any encouragement that comes will be because the Holy Spirit inspired me. I take no credit for this, but will rejoice when it happens."

Out of all of the possible titles for this book, I chose *Intergalactic Dancing* because dancing is one of my favourite types of worship.

Praise his name with dancing, accompanied by drums and lyre.[1]

He delights in the dance. He calls His people to dance.

Some of these entries have been expanded for the purpose of making them clearer for the reader. I make no apologies for the repetition of phrases, "as I was reflecting", "I had a sense that", "while I was meditating". These inspirations and reflections are not set up in any particular chronological order. Also, words that are in italics are foreign words and Scriptures. Words that are in bold print are for my own personal emphasis. Often the name of Jesus will appear in its Hebrew form *Yeshua*.

The beauty of a book of this kind is that you can pick it up even if you just have five minutes or so. You will find something to inspire you and something to reflect on. You may even go back to some of these entries more than once. Drink deeply and be refreshed! You know this for sure, when you refresh others, you get refreshed yourself.

As you begin to see how God speaks to me, you will begin to hear Him for yourself. This is one of my prayers. For me yet, it has never been an audible voice, but a deep knowing, an inner voice! I have heard Him in my quiet times as well as in the middle of the practical happenings of life. He speaks 24/7. His name is The Word! He is speaking to all of us, at all times in everyday matters. By His Spirit, He is inviting you to learn to listen. I hope that you will begin to see some of the different ways that God speaks. So, in some way, this book is about you and me and how we are continually learning to discern God's voice.

Another prayer is that hidden somewhere in these pages you will be renewed and encouraged. My highest hope is that you would see Jesus, the Light of the World, the Living Word, the Messiah of Israel, the soon and coming King, the Ruler of the Universe and invite Him into your life!

If in any way, one or several of these reflections have blessed you, please let me know. Go to www.intergalacticdancing.com or cg@intergalacticdancing.com

DEDICATION

I dedicate this book to God's greater honour and glory, to my husband Bill, our sons, Paul, Ron, Steve, Ray and their families, to my relatives and friends, former students, former interns and all those who have graced my life till now.

1 The Purple Skirt

Often I have reflected on the fact that God is the ultimate Redeemer. I have also shared this truth with many people. His desire is to redeem every thought, word, deed, and person on this planet. This is how He did it for me on one particular occasion.

One day, a lady at our church, who usually wore quite expensive clothing, was wearing a purple skirt that was not particularly flattering for her: neither were my thoughts about her.

A few years later, I was visiting my mother who was going through her closet and she offered me some clothes: among them a beautiful **purple skirt.** After I had accepted it, she told me that it had been given to her by that very same lady that I had the negative thoughts about!!! The skirt had come full circle: from critical thoughts to my ownership. God was mercifully giving me an opportunity to have my thoughts redeemed. I repented for my sinful thinking and gratefully enjoyed the beautiful purple skirt for a season or two.

Thank you, Lord, for giving me an opportunity to have these thoughts redeemed by Your love. You are always challenging us:

Finally, brethren, whatsoever things are true, whatsoever things are honest, whatsoever things are just, whatsoever things are pure, whatsoever things are lovely, whatsoever things are of good report; if there be any virtue, and if t here be any praise, think on these things.[1]

2 Microphone to the Universe

As I was dozing off to sleep, I heard these words, "**Microphone to the universe!**" I saw myself and others taking turns speaking into this microphone, quoting God's Word and making godly declarations that would reverberate throughout the universe. Amazing! The microphone could be any object of our choice, or no object at all: it was all done by faith and faith alone.

If you don't believe it, don't worry, it won't happen. If you have faith for it, believe that God will use the words you send out to change the atmosphere around you and to make glorious changes on this planet. It is faith that always pleases God.

What is faith? It is the confident assurance that something we want is going to happen. It is the certainty that what we hope for is waiting for us, even though we cannot see it up ahead.[1]

As the rain and snow come down from heaven and stay upon the ground to water the earth, and cause the grain to grow and to produce seed for the farmer and bread or the hungry, so also is my Word. I send it out and it always accomplishes all I want it too, and prosper everywhere I send it.[2]

3 From a Teaching on the Radio

When we look at each other, we sometimes see one another's faults or perhaps we see each other as a "field of dirt". When Jesus looks at us, He never sees the "dirt," He only sees the treasure buried in the field. The Book of Matthew illustrates:

The kingdom of the heavens is like a treasure a man discovered in the field. In his excitement, he sold everything he owned to get enough money to buy the field – and get the treasure too.[1]

We are of such value to Jesus that when the field went up on the auction block, He thought of the hidden treasure and said, "I'll pay for it even with My Blood."

It is time for us to value the preciousness of each person.

Let's be like Jesus and start recognizing the treasure that is within us as well as in others. Jesus, please give me eyes to recognize the unique beauty in everyone I meet.

The words of Psalm 139 remind us that we are very precious to God.

You made all the delicate inner parts of my body, and knit them together in my mother's womb. Thank You for making me so wonderfully complex! It is amazing to think about. Your workmanship is marvellous, and how well I know it. You were there while I was being formed in utter seclusion. You saw me before I was born and scheduled each day of my life before I began to breathe. Everyday was recorded in your book! How precious it is Lord to realize that you are thinking about me constantly! I can't even count how many times a day your thoughts turn towards me.[2]

4 pH Level 8

One morning after an all-night prayer meeting, I checked my **pH level** when I got home and was astounded to see that it was 8, which was very positive. A balanced pH is usually around 7. Lower pH levels represent a more acidic body: in this state, the body is busy dealing with toxins, and a person is subject to sickness. As the pH progresses toward 8 it means that the body is more alkaline and healthier. An alkaline body can easily protect itself against germs and infections. I realized that being in God's Presence makes us healthy. Sickness does not thrive in an alkaline body. By God's glorious grace, I had attained a place of divine immunity.

We are told that Moses lived to be 120 years of age. His vision was still great and so was his physical strength. Moses had spent two 40-day periods in God's Presence on Mount Sinai. Scripture conveys that he was in the glory of God. In the glory, there is no diminishing of strength or aging!

Recently, I tested a salt solution and watched it immediately register a pH of 8! Then I remembered why Jesus called us, "the salt of the earth."[1] We are to bring healing to those around us!

5 The Word is a Sword

The Word of the Lord is a sword. Sometimes we must plunge that sword into the mountain of the Lord and hang on to it for dear life so that we don't fall over the cliff. It is possible to fall off the mountain at any level, if we are not grounded in the Word.

This impression came to me after reading Rick Joyner's book, *The Final Quest*. [1] As we thrust this sword, and learn to move it well, it becomes a "joy-stick" and gives us power in the "game" of life.

6 Jesus our 'Burden-Bearer'

I think all of our problems have handles on them. The purpose of these handles is so that we can seize our problems and turn them over to **Jesus our 'Burden-Bearer'**. No human was ever created to carry burdens, but Jesus did this for us when He died on the Cross. Thank you, Jesus!

He is despised and rejected by men, A Man of sorrows and acquainted with grief. And we hid, as it were, our faces from Him; He was despised, and we did not esteem Him. Surely He has borne our griefs and carried our sorrows; yet we esteemed Him stricken, Smitten by God, and afflicted. But He was wounded for our transgressions, He was bruised for our iniquities; the chastisement for our peace was upon Him, and by His stripes we are healed. All we like sheep have gone astray; we have turned, every one, to his own way; And the LORD *has laid on Him the iniquity of us all.*[1]

7 Cleansing Water

When we drink a lot of water, our natural body must have an outlet for it or we'd burst. God created one! When we drink in Living Water it must have an outlet too: rivers of living water flowing from our innermost being, reviving, cleansing, and refreshing those around us.

For the Scriptures declare that rivers of living water shall flow from the inmost being of anyone who believes in me.[1]

8 Women of War

The Holy Spirit had been prompting me to get the video, *Joan of Arc* which I had seen at the theatre when I was in grade four. It had a tremendous impact on me then, and it did when I watched it again. The next day, one of our sons and his wife gave me a beautifully framed poem called; *The Warrior* about the women who do spiritual warfare. Tonight, I watched a video which a friend 'just happened' to lend me, called *Hannah's War*.

O Lord, you are putting valiant, bold, courageous women of integrity before my eyes. Please cause me to become all that you have created me to be! I have already enlisted in Your army and have been in boot camp and specialized training for years. May You be glorified in me. The next night one of our pastors taught on **spiritual warfare**.

9 God's Book Report About My Life

While attending Windsor Christian Fellowship, Pastor Rick Ciaramitaro gave an excellent teaching on the Book of Remembrance mentioned in the Book of Malachi. He asked us to answer this question: "What is **God's book report about my life?**" When I got home, the Holy Spirit gave me the following poem.

God: Connie, Connie, what did you find?
Connie: It says, O Lord that I am kind
I see there written much beauty too!
You amaze me Lord: Your mercy's ever new
People who love me have always said nice things
So why should I be surprised as the God of love sings
You sing of my life with Your voice, O God
You rejoice over me and tread where I've trod
But my name as Connie I do not see
I see Constance written as big as can be
My name in letters large to read
Is not that to me people heed
But you have trusted me to share
The name of Jesus with love and care
After my name I see numbers— so many in all
They're the souls that have answered Your heavenly call-
They're souls now snatched from the fires of hell
Because I love you Lord and on my knees I fell.
What else have You written
What else is in Your Book?
God: You've love both Gentile and Jew
Therefore great rewards await you!

10 Leading to the Lord

I had the joy of **leading a young man to the Lord** who was a step brother to some of my former students. There was absolutely no resistance in him. The Holy Spirit had prepared him well. The bookstore at our church gave him a Student's Study Bible and a few small booklets to help along on his new journey.

Father God, thank You for the church's generosity to him. Father, You are becoming a father to that young man, because You are a father to those who need one. Hopefully, You will find a good school for this handsome young man. By the authority that You have given me, I reverse every curse and negative word ever spoken over him in the name of Jesus and by the power of the Blood of the Lamb!

11 Enlarge My Tent

Isaiah 54 says, "***Enlarge my tent** O Lord!*"[1]

Stretch me whichever way You desire. Cause me never to walk away from You! You are faithful to Your covenants to love, protect, provide and accept me! Thank You.

I desperately need You, Lord. Let me love, protect, provide and accept others as You do for me. Cause me to love with Your love and not my own selfish love. I renew my pledge to You that You are Lord over every area of my life! I look to You and Your Word to sustain me. Give me courage not to be overcome by my circumstance.

With God's help I declare that I will love with God's love!

You have heard that it was said, 'You shall love your neighbour and hate your enemy.' But I say to you, love your enemies, bless those who curse you, do good to those who hate you, and pray for those who spitefully use you and persecute you... For if you love those who love you, what reward have you? Do not even the tax collectors do the same? [2]

12 God My Provider

God has been providing for me in a magnificent way.

Just before I retired from teaching, with a very small pension, I sensed that God wanted me to buy a car from my mother's friend. God knew that I hated debt and I really didn't have the money for the car. However, I sensed that He wanted to do this for me. The sense was so strong, that by faith I purchased this wonderful vehicle. It was the shade of green that I wanted and had very low mileage. Because I felt that the Lord would pay for it, I arranged the loan payments to be very small, so that He would have an opportunity to pay for it in full! After having made two small payments, a fair amount of money came to me from an unexpected source and it covered the cost of my loan. Halleluiah! God also provider a buyer for my previous car, which sold at a very good price!

He guards all that is mine.[1]

In return, I purchased personalized plates for the car. They read, *KADOSH,* which is Hebrew for Holy, because He is a holy God. I wanted to advertise for Him.

13 Conduits of His Presence

Each of us is a channel: a **conduit of God's Presence!** We may be the size of a sipping straw, a garden hose, a pipe or a culvert. We all have the capacity to let God flow through us—our capacity and anointing can continually be enlarged. As we converge in the same place with unity of heart and mind, His Presence is released. We have the potential, not only to water our cities and nations but also to create rivers of life for all to swim in.

For the Scriptures declare that rivers of living water shall flow from the inmost being of anyone who believes in me.[1]

14 Entire Galaxies

A man was taken up to the Throne of God. There he saw angels in heaven that had been given charge **over entire galaxies**. Those angels 'envied' the responsibility that the other angels had who ruled over one single saint of God: so awesome is His Presence within us! They would much rather have charge over one single Christian than **an entire galaxy**. God has decided to dwell in man, and the value He has put on us, we cannot begin to fathom. Do you know what He showed that man? One day in the life of a believer has more significance than the entire lifetime of many of history's greatest conquerors because one day in our life has eternal value and consequences.[1]

You are of God, little children, and have overcome them, because He who is in you is greater than he who is in the world.[2]

15 An Ocean of Gratitude

"Make thankfulness your sacrifice to God."[1] I see myself standing on the **ocean shores of gratitude** and each wave brings something else for which I am so thankful!

1. **My salvation** and all that goes with it: healing, deliverance, protection, provision, and prosperity.
2. The power of the **Blood of Jesus** for abundance, acceptance, blessings, forgiveness, healing, glory, life, the new man, His righteousness. [2] Along with this: His Body and His Blood in **Communion.**
3. **The Word of God**: my daily bread; my sustenance.
4. **My family**: my dear husband Bill. We have been married for 48 years; our four wonderful sons, Paul, Ron, Steve, and Ray, who by God's grace are all men of integrity as well as their gracious wives: Joy, Kristen, and Lyndi; our

19 remarkable grand children and our two great-grand sons and a third great grandson on the way.

Your wife shall be contented in your home. And look at all those children! There they sit around the dinner table as vigorous and healthy as young olive trees. That is God's reward to those who reverence and trust him.[3]

Indeed I am a blessed woman! It would take another book to give true justice to the family that God has created for me. My gratitude for my family is inestimable!

5. **Extended family** members and my many, many **friends** who have celebrated good times with me and also stood by me in the hours of difficulty. Throughout my life I have always considered both groups as generous gifts from God.

6. **Prophetic ministry** that has enriched my life with so much encouragement.

7. The passion that You have given me for all that pertains to **Israel**: her God, her book, her people and her land. This also includes my numerous trips to Israel and the ministry of prayer and encouragement given to me while I am there.

8. The **gifting, the call and the destiny** over my life!

9. For all of our **family gatherings,** and the love and harmony that we experience at those times.

10. For my church family, for Pastor Gertruda Armaly, who seeks Your face before any and all decisions she makes, and for all other pastors in our church: a very godly group!

11. For the intercessors that meet every week at Antioch Christian Ministries who challenge me to keep meeting with God. Through them I hear God's heart beating.

12. For all former **students and the interns of Antioch School of Destiny.**

13. For my 16 years of involvement in **street ministry** in the City of Windsor and for the unity and fellowship with all those involved in this ministry. A touch of heaven!
14. For Pastor Bob and Leona Halpenny and the ministry of *Bet Tefillah.* [This is Hebrew for 'House of Prayer'.] By God's loving grace we have been meeting every other week for 15 years now for the sole purpose of blessing Israel and praying for her. Each person in that group is a precious gift to me.
15. For my **computer** and all of the great things that I receive on it and all the wonderful things that I also get to send out.
16. For my **spiritual growth** as an overcomer: this fruit is growing and becoming more mature. It is part of the "the peace of God, which surpasses all understanding."[4]
17. For the many **cards, letters and notes** that I receive throughout the years as well as those that I send.
18. For my **excellent health**: a cherished possession.
19. This list is as **endless** as the waves of the ocean and I want to stay grateful, but I know for sure that for all eternity I will be worshipping Him not so much for things, as much as for the beauty of His majesty and the glory around His Throne. Lord, please help me to stay in an attitude of gratitude for Your honour and glory! I offer thanksgiving with my whole heart. You are precious to me. Amen!

16 It Was Worth It

I burned my wrist while cooking the Thanksgiving turkey. Afterwards I saw the scar. It reminded me of the day and the joy we all had together and I say, "It was worth it!"

When the Father looks upon all the scars and bruises that His Son Jesus endured for us, it is always a reminder that Jesus did it "for the joy that was set before Him"[1] and He says, "**It was worth it!**" Because of Jesus' sacrifice on the Cross, He caused me to become 'worth it!' He also saw the multitude that would choose to boldly follow Him in the future: His sacrifice was not in vain. It is my pledge to live in such a way that He will have pleasure in my life because of all that He endured for me.

17 Intergalactic Dancing

The very first prophetic word that I received just a few days after my retirement from teaching was, "I will restore the joy of the **dance**." After that, more prophetic words concerning the dance just kept flowing. The following are a few of them:

"I see pink ballerina slippers on your feet. Continue **dancing** before the Lord. Continue worshipping this way. It delights His heart."

"You are on top of a mountain **dancing.** There are strings attached to your hands and feet that reach to heaven."

"You are wearing golden slippers. As you walk and as you **dance** you are a warrior, taking ground for God's Kingdom. You are treading on the enemy. Every place that your feet tread: the enemy has dread."

"Your **dancing** refreshes the intercessors. You are an intercessor for intercessors. You go around and pour oil in their lamps so that their fires won't go out. Your **dance** is worship and warfare."

"I'm thinking of the old worldly song, "I Could Have Danced All Night," and my daughter you will **dance** all night! You will **dance** before many people! Your movements with your hands, your steps and even your rhythm are all prophetic and they are directed by Me! You please Me, my daughter! You are a **worshipper and a warrior** and I love your praises."

"God has released **angels to dance around you!**"

"Keep **dancing** before the Lord! Keep **dancing** before the Lord! You are slaying many giants! You are slaying many giants! You are slaying many giants!"

"When you **dance** you drive the devil nuts because you are saying, "nah, nah, nah, nah, nah, nah." Your freedom is worship.

You increase encouragement for the intercessors and you encourage people to worship."

"A few weeks ago when you were **dancing** up front without a banner, I opened my eyes and saw a beautiful angel **dancing** and keeping rhythm with you."

"I saw you **dancing** with your scarf in your hand and there was an angel on either side of you and they were doing what you did. Then, when you came to the other side of the sanctuary, two more angels came and **danced** with you and protected you. As you bowed, two more angels bowed and worshipped with you. The features of the last two angels were different from the rest and they were wearing white, but the lace on their gowns was beige. Now there were six angels with you. It was beautiful and pleased the Lord."

When I used to see myself **dancing** with the Lord, I imagined both of us in a huge, beautiful ballroom, a palace type, maybe something like the one described in the Book of Esther.

The decorations were green, white and blue, fastened with purple ribbons tied to silver rings embedded in gold and silver benches stood on pavements of black, red, white and yellow marble.[1]

Soon, I realized that I was causing Him to **dance** on my turf: here on earth and in my limited environment. Then, I sensed that the Holy Spirit was inviting me to **dance** with the Lord in **His** territory: the universe— **dancing** through the galaxies. *"...*

The LORD's throne is in heaven...[2]

The heaven even the heavens are the LORD's.[3]

He loves to twirl me around on His own dance floor then He creates the music there.

When the morning stars sang together, And all the sons of God shouted for joy? [4]

Then, the Holy Spirit revealed to me that my **dancing** was now "**Inter-galactic!**"
I dance for an audience of One—God!

18 Surprising Sources of Encouragement

Yesterday, I was feeling very wimpy with regard to my faith-walk. I believe that the voice of the accuser was very loud, and forgive me, Lord, I had been listening to it! Today, the Lord used two unsaved people to confirm my growth in Him.

A former swimming instructor came to me in the corridor and made a reference to some encouraging words that I had given him last week. With tears in his eyes, he said, "You really saw me like no one else has." Thank You, Lord, for continuing the work that You are doing in him.

The other was a young man that I had encountered a few weeks ago while doing street ministry in the downtown area. When we met again he commented, "When I am with you I feel so peaceful and light." Lord, You see the call on this young man's life. More angels around him please, and Lord, thank You for keeping me encouraged on life's journey from **surprising sources of encouragement**.

19 Feeling the Anointing

It is not too often that I literally **feel the anointing** of God. By faith, I know that He is here and that He is active and moving on my behalf. I was looking at a book-table in the foyer of our church. When I reached out my hand to pick up, *Dancing in the Anointing*,[1] I felt an anointing run through my arm. So, I realized that this was the book for me. It proved to be a confirmation of what I had felt and it was a real blessing to me!

20 I Am My Beloved's and My Beloved is Mine

Last night I slept at Mom's. In the morning, she gave me a ring that she had purchased at the Messiah Conference the previous year. She said that it was too big for her. The inscription on the ring was in Hebrew and read: "*I am My Beloved's and My Beloved is Mine.*"[1] I was thrilled and very appreciative of her gift. When I arrived at home, a book that I had ordered from the same conference had arrived. The title of that wonderful book: *I Am My Beloved's.*[2]

Thank You, Lord, You really want me to get this message that I am Yours and You are mine. I am so grateful for Your love!

21 Sowing Seeds of Eternal Life

I met a couple last night that I had not seen in years. Several years previous to this I had taught their sons. To one of them I had given a Bible. They thanked me profusely for praying them into the Kingdom and for having given their son a Bible as a gift. It was this Bible that opened their eyes to the truth of Messiah Jesus and now they are born-again.

When I gave out Bibles to my students it was always in faith that they or someone in their home would read it and yield to God. Today, I saw the fruit of the seed that was planted.

22 Plans in Writing

During my private prayer time, the Lord reminded me that He is the One who had written out the Ten Commandments for Moses and also He is the One who had given King David the blueprints for the Temple. So I prayed, "Oh Lord, please give me some of your **plans in writing**!"

"I did", said the Lord, "Open it up and read My plans for you: they are written in a book called The Bible."

23 Married With Children

When a person with children remarries, among other things, he or she is looking for a spouse who will not only love him or her, but also love the children.

Our Father in Heaven is looking for a Bride for His Son: one who will share His vision for all of His lost children, who need to be nurtured and loved back into wholeness. We cannot say that we truly love Him without being committed to His Passion for the lost. It will cost us; it already cost His Son everything — even His life on the Cross.

24 Water on a Duck's Back

Have you ever watched some birds prepare their wings before rain? They rub some sort of oil on their wings from secretions under their wings so that they become more water repellent. I believe that God's anointing is something like that.

The word anointing literally means to rub with fat or 'to consecrate with oil'. [1] The anointing is like the oil from heaven that helps us to function in the things that God has called us to do, as well to help us to take our problems and slip them off of our backs. Scripture says:

And it shall come to pass in that day, that his burden shall be taken away from off thy shoulder, and his yoke from off thy neck, and the yoke shall be destroyed because of the anointing. [2]

I was reflecting on how our problems can weigh us down, and how the anointing can take care of things, when suddenly the words to this ridiculously simple song came to me:

Water on a duck's back
Quack! Quack! Quack!
Water on a duck's back
Quack! Quack! Quack!
Water on a duck's back
Quack! Quack! Quack!
God's anointing makes it like that!

O Lord, may Your anointing on me cause me to slide my problems onto You: I am too weak to carry them. I need You, O Lord!

Jesus calls us to come to Him if we are weary and tired. He wants to give us rest. He is meek [not weak] and He will allow us to be yoked together with Him as a team. Every thing about Jesus speaks of rest and gentleness. Jesus meek and humble of heart, make our hearts just like Yours!

25 Racing on the Runway or Lift-Off?

Following after the Holy Spirit leads to life and peace, but following after the old nature leads to death.[1]

When reflecting on this verse, Holy Spirit showed me that when we are led by our old natures we are like cars on the run-way at the airport, who think we are planes: we go too fast, often ending up in a crash, but we never have a lift-off.

When we are led by the Holy Spirit, we are like the plane! Yes, we have wheels too and we do roll on the run-way, but there is a glorious lift-off and we soar in His peace and love! God wants to carry us up onto eagles' wings, and bring us to Himself.

You have seen what I did… and how I brought you to myself as though on eagle's wings.[2]

26 Money to Give Away

Today, I was surprised to receive a large gift of money. Thank You, Lord, hoorah! And Lord, I had told you that whatever money I received above pension or salary, I would give half of it away. So, thank You for making provision for me to be able to give 'like a rich lady'.

*But seek ye first the kingdom of God, and his righteousness; and **all these things shall be added unto you**.* [1]

27 The X-wing Fighter

Through a close friend I received a very encouraging word. He described an **X-wing fighter** to me that the Air Force has. It cannot be flown without a computer because the pilot's normal reactions and senses bring the plane out of balance every time. Why? The pilot is trying to fly a new design with former skills. Since that time, my prayer has been, "Please fly my plane, O Lord and take control of my life!"

A few days later at our church, a man with a prophetic gift declared that we needed to 'allow God to change our course'. This word tied in perfectly with "**Fly my plane, O Lord!**" I don't want God as my co-pilot: I need Him as my pilot.

But they that wait upon the Lord *shall renew their strength. They shall mount up with wings like eagles, they shall run and not be weary; they shall walk and not faint.*[1]

28 Thank You for the Hard Times

Through my morning devotional called, *Sapphires* by Jonathan Cahn [1] I was a challenged to write a poem thanking God even for my difficulties. This was in October 2003, and this is what the Holy Spirit gave me.

Thank You for the hard times
The hard times
The hard times
Thank You for the prison house
That You designed for me!

Like Joseph stuck in Egypt
Like Jesus on planet earth
Obedience I learned through suffering, not mirth.
The pain has prompted seeking
And a hunger after You
Nothing else could have caused me
To be true to You
Stability I sought, as though an answered prayer
But it came only in knowing
That You were always there

Endurance to conquer
Came not overnight
But through the daily battles
Where You taught me how to fight.

For long-suffering I never asked
But its fruit delighted You
And so for years You guarded me
In all that I went through
The pain was always awful
But You always have been there
Through it all I came to know

Of Your tremendous care

Nothing else but suffering
Could have purified this life!
No! Nothing on this planet
And nothing in this place
Could ever have brought me closer
To your redeeming grace.
And so…

Thank You for the hard times
The hard timesThe hard times
Thank you for the prison house
That you designed for me!

29 The Dignified Bride

The Holy Spirit was reminding me of how inappropriate it
would look to see a young woman in a very expensive bridal
gown, with her hair sticking out all over, a cigarette in her hand,
slouched on a couch etc. We would think that she didn't know she
was a bride—a lack of suitable dignity.

This can be true with all of us!

The Lord adorns me every day with a new robe of righteousness—more lovely than the one from the day before. It is relevant
for me to carry myself with the dignity of a bride.

Let us be glad and rejoice, and give honour to him: for the
marriage of the Lamb is come, and his wife **hath made**
herself ready. *And to her was granted that she should be*
arrayed in fine linen, clean and white: for the fine linen is the
righteousness of saints.[1]

30 Luminescent

After ministering on the streets for a few hours, the Holy Spirit reminded me why angels are so **luminescent:** because they live in God's Presence and they are always ministering to the lost, just as we were doing.

Are not all angels ministering spirits sent to serve those who will inherit salvation? [1]

My friend noticed that my face was shining and said that it was actually glowing! More of You, Lord! Let there be no veil like Moses had to wear please.

*The LORD bless thee, and keep thee: **The LORD make his face shine upon thee**, and be gracious unto thee: The LORD lift up his countenance upon thee, and give thee peace.* [2]

31 Suntan or Son-tan?

When we lie in the sun for a while it is beneficial for us. If we are there longer, we tan or burn and it becomes obvious that our skin has been changed. When we are in the Presence of the Son of God we don't need to do anything, just receive from Him. We change, and in time, it becomes obvious to others too.

Return to your rest, O my soul, for the LORD has dealt bountifully with you.[1]

32 Guarding our Boundaries

After Chuck Pierce's prophetic visit to our church I purchased his book, *Ridding Your Home of Spiritual Darkness*.[1] Following his advice I prayer-walked the boundaries of our property, covered it with the Blood of Jesus, and declared a canopy of praise over the whole area. In accordance with his suggestion, I wrote Scripture passages on small pieces of paper and buried them where the Spirit showed me. They are as follows:

On the Northeast Corner
No evil shall befall you, nor shall any plague come near your dwelling; for He shall give His angels charge over you, to keep you in all your ways.[2]

He who has an ear, let him hear what the Spirit says to the churches. To him who overcomes I will give some of the hidden manna to eat. And I will give him a white stone, and on the stone a new name written which no one knows except him who receives it.[3]

On the Northwest Corner
I will say of the LORD, "He is my refuge and my fortress; My God, in Him I will trust. [4]

To him who overcomes I will grant to sit with Me on My throne, as I also overcame and sat down with My Father on His throne.[5]

On the Southwest Corner
Because he has set his love upon Me, therefore I will deliver him; I will set him on high, because he has known My name. He shall call upon Me, and I will answer him; I will be with him in trouble; I will deliver him and honour him. With long life I will satisfy him, and show him My salvation.[6]

He who overcomes, I will make him a pillar in the temple of My God, and he shall go out no more. I will write on him the name of My God and the name of the city of My God, the New Jerusalem, which comes down out of heaven from My God. And I will write on him My new name.[7]

On the Southeast Corner
He who dwells in the secret place of the Most High shall abide under the shadow of the Almighty. I will say of the L<small>ORD</small>, "He is my refuge and my fortress; my God, in Him I will trust." Surely He shall deliver you from the snare of the fowler and from the perilous pestilence.[8]

To him who overcomes I will give to eat from the tree of life, which is in the midst of the Paradise of God.[9]

Each corner has a portion of Psalm 91 and also some of the promises to overcomers found in Revelations 2 and 3. Many of these are for protection, enlargement and courage.

For He has strengthened the bars of your gates; He has blessed your children within you.[10]

33 Cancer Healed

A few of us met in the home of a friend, having served on the *March for Jesus* committee for our city. By this time, I had developed a large melanoma across my nose. It had been growing for a month or so. It was black, sore, spreading, and three layers of make-up could no longer conceal it. After my friends anointed me with oil and prayed for healing—I went home. That evening, the growth appeared different. It looked lose. I gently touched it, and the whole black growth lifted right off of my nose without any resistance. Underneath was fresh pink skin.

You have been good to me, O Lord! From ages ago, You have revealed Yourself as the God who heals.

I am the Lord that healeth [heals] thee.[1]

No weapon formed against you shall prosper… This is the heritage of the servants of the L<small>ORD</small>.[2]

And cancer is certainly a weapon formed against us! There is no cancer in heaven!

34 Flying Safely

Recently, while I was flying home from California, I made the following declaration:

"I always fly in the safest part of the plane!"

You may ask, "Where's that?"

"Wherever I sit!"

In Psalm 91, He has promised to send His angels to protect us wherever we go!

35 The Sea of Galilee

A reflection and prayer after listening to one of Jonathan Cahn's teachings: "O Lord, cause me to continue to be like the Sea of Galilee and receive my whole life from on high."

The Sea of Galilee's source is from the melted snow and rain on Mount Hermon. Therefore, its water is always fresh, clean, and full of life. The Sea of Galilee flows into the Jordan River, which then flows down into the Dead Sea.

Allow me, O God, to have the strength to continue to pour out my life into others who might sometimes be like the Dead Sea: not giving or returning life; just content to receive!

Jesus said,

But I say to you, love your enemies, bless those who curse you, do good to those who hate you, and pray for those who spitefully use you and persecute you, that you may be sons of your Father in heaven; for He makes His sun riseon the evil and on the good, and sends rain on the just and on the unjust.[1]

36 A Poem To the King

My heart is overflowing with a beautiful thought! I will write a lovely poem to the King, for I am full of words.[1]

The author of Psalm 45 declared that his "tongue is the pen of a ready writer."[2]

In May of 2007 as I reflected on this verse, I felt prompted by the Holy Spirit to do just as the psalmist had done: write **a poem to the King**!

How lovely is Your dwelling place O Lord!
You have put a longing in my heart for reward:
To be with You!
To see Your face!
To be in that place – that garden
Prepared from the foundations of the world
I long to look at You
As You're seated on Your Throne.
I long to bow before You
And worship You alone.

There's none like You, O Father
And there's no one like Your Son
Your love- the love between the two of You
Is poured each day into my heart anew
By Your Spirit ever true to You!
I long for You!
I long for more of You!
I long to dance with angels
And all of the redeemed!

The Blood was shed
And we are led
Into Your Presence – forevermore! Amen!

37 Teflon

A friend and I were having lunch. The topic of offenses came up when she very wisely said, "We need to be Teflon-coated — nothing can stick to us!" Paul wrote:

I therefore, the prisoner of the Lord, beseech you to walk worthy of the calling with which you were called, with all lowliness and gentleness, with longsuffering, bearing with one another in love, endeavouring to keep the unity of the Spirit in the bond of peace.[1]

38 One New Man

*At that time you were without Christ, **being aliens from the commonwealth of Israel** and strangers from the covenants of promise, having no hope and without God in the world. But now in Christ Jesus you who once were far off have been brought near by the blood of Christ. For he is our peace, who hath made both one, and hath broken down the middle wall of partition between us; Having abolished in his flesh the enmity, even the law of commandments contained in ordinances; for to make in himself of twain [two] **one new man**, so making peace.*[1]

God is eager for this one new man to come forth!

As I was reflecting on these words, I pictured Christ as the Head in heaven above us. Below the head was half of a Jewish body full of Stars of David, and on the other side, half of a Christian body full of crosses. Through countless centuries each half has been moving in its own direction, most often with little observation. We are of the generation, I believe, that will see the fullness of the Body of Messiah become the One New Man in glorious and obedient surrender under the unity of Jesus Christ our Head, the Messiah of Israel.

39 From Sumac to Oak Tree

One evening, the Lord gave me this poem:

Not like the sumac that is so small
But like the oak so straight and tall
Resplendent in crimson that doesn't fade
Shining brightly with My glory arrayed
You are My oak of righteousness
You are my forest of delight!
You'll need no defense but Mine
And I'll be with you all the time.

Isaiah declares:

For God has planted them like strong and graceful **oaks** *for his own glory.*[1]

40 Handles for Sale

Before I begin studying a new topic about God, I usually have some related knowledge about it. Often, the initial knowledge seems to be like pots on the stove that have no handles, and that makes it hard to 'do' anything with that knowledge.

While studying, the Holy Spirit is reminding me that study is like "buying handles' for the pots to make better use of what I already know. Now, I say, "**Handles for sale**! Who will buy handles?" With handles we can make better use of the pots we already have and we can pour our knowledge into other containers.

The Word of God encourages us to keep studying so that we have a good understanding of truth.

41 God's Presence

I was reflecting on words that I once heard Richard Wurmbrandt's say, "Lord, You said that You cause the sun to shine on the just and the unjust and here I am in the underground concentration camp (for fourteen years), so who am I to You, Lord? There is NO sunshine here at all!" The Lord replied to him, "I want you to be the sunshine to those that are here".

Then the Lord reminded me that He would manifest Himself to those who obey Him.

He that has my commandments and keeps them, he it is that loves me; but he that loves me shall be loved by my Father, and I will love him and will **manifest myself to him.**[1]

There are so many people in our church who experience His manifest Presence, and I don't in the same way. Thus, the enemy has used this as a point of accusation to me. So then, like Richard Wurmbrandt I asked, "Then who am I to You, Lord, because I do love you and I do obey You?" But this evening, I believe God was speaking to my spirit and saying, "I trust you to bring My manifest Presence to others!" So be it!

42 Grocery Shopping for Others

While reflecting on how well we have been fed spiritually at our conferences through Antioch Christian Ministries, the former Woodslee Prayer Community Church, I heard a voice within me say, "Connie, you're not coming to conferences to feed yourself only ; but rather, you are **grocery shopping for others!**"

43 Canada, Israel and the Bridge in Between

My 60th birthday! Thank You, Lord, for all these years! As a birthday gift from God my request was:

Ask of Me and I will give the nations as an inheritance for you.[1]

I have been asking Him for a specific gift each year for the last five years. So this year, Lord, I ask for **Canada, Israel and the bridge in between** them.

During our time of intercession at the Woodslee Prayer Community Church, between nine a.m. and noon, we prayed that day mainly for Canada and Israel. We understood that Israel needed prayer and that we would be blessed when we prayed for Israel.

After our gathering, two friends from another city who were present at the prayer meeting came to me in the parking lot and gave me much material regarding the Twelve Tribes of Israel. I was immediately blessed.

Another super blessing was this: my sons and their wives threw a surprise party for me for 60 people in a big hall. They were most generous. It was a lovely and remarkably memorable evening. How blessed I am to have such a glorious, beautiful family—and all those relatives, grandchildren and friends! The surprise of it all took quite a while to get over. When the Lord blesses, He uses other people. It was wonderful to have those people be family.

44 Prepare the Way

This morning as I was writing a love-letter to Jesus I reminded Him that I previously declared that I would not die in the wilderness, but rather, as the Song of Songs says,

Who is this coming up from the wilderness, leaning upon her beloved? [1]

I had also asked the Lord once again for a Hebrew soul.

In His very brief and beautiful letter to me He finished it by saying, "And watch what I will do for you today!" At 11: 30 a.m. I was to meet a pastor and his wife who invited me, as God would have it, to become a board member for a ministry supporting Israel, called, **Prepare the Way** Ministries. Also, that morning, the reading in the devotional called "Our Daily Bread" was entitled, 'Board of Directors'! Truly amazing and very confirming!

Through this pastor's request I see the fulfillment of many of the prophetic words that have been spoken over me regarding Israel, and also an answer to my birthday prayer regarding Canada, Israel and the bridge in between. To make the confirmation even more solid, I received a card in the mail from the Jewish National Fund from a Jewish lady that I had never met. She had a tree planted in Israel for me as an act of appreciation for the letter that I had written to The Windsor Star newspaper in support of Israel. Surely, the heavens are opening up over me, and I am blessed!

45 Healthy Body–Healthy Bride

Fresh water, fresh fruits and roughage/fibre clean out our bodies. In the same way, God is going to use the river of life, the fresh fruit of His Spirit and roughage: hard times, trials and persecutions to clean up His Bride.

Count it all joy when you fall into various trials, knowing that the testing of your faith produces patience. But let patience have its perfect work, that you may be perfect and complete, lacking nothing.[1]

46 A Parable: Baking a Cake

The Lord revealed this to me a long time ago, but I feel to write it down now so that I won't forget it: paper doesn't forget!

When I am making a cake from scratch and I put eggs into the bowl and begin to beat them, if someone were to come into the room and ask what I am doing, I wouldn't say, "I'm beating eggs" but rather, "I'm **baking a cake**." As a cook who has experience and recognizes the beginning from the end of cakes, I am making a declaration not based on circumstances, or any senses, but rather based on the knowledge of the end product. No one would dispute my saying it either, because of their own personal knowledge. Even when other ingredients are put into the bowl, my answer would still be the same, "I'm baking a cake." When all the ingredients are in and the cake is in the oven, my declaration would always be the same. Although we know that, at that time, the 'cake' neither looks like, tastes like nor has the consistency of a cake. The end product has determined the name throughout the whole process.

So too with us as 'saints': God gives us this title the moment we invite Jesus into our hearts as Lord and Saviour. At this point we don't fully reflect His character, His nature, or His high call. Yet, He still calls us 'saints'. Even when other ingredients get added; the fruit and gifts of the Holy Spirit, we most often don't look like, or feel like a saint. God has declared that WE ARE His saints. He tells us that when He appears we'll be just like Him! He is appearing to us now in many ways, through His Word, teachings, the work of His Spirit, through other saints, mentors, etc. So the 'saint' will become fully baked and mature. Fear Not!

47 Role Models

During worship, the Holy Spirit encouraged me to ask this question to people at a later time: "Have any of the following people influenced your life? Jesus? Paul? Peter? John? Abraham?

Jacob? Moses? Elijah? Elisha? David? Esther? Mary? Nehemiah? Isaiah? Jeremiah? "

If so, you have had Hebrews — Israelites — Jews as **role models**!

I will make you (Israel) a light to the nations of the world to bring my salvation to them.[1]

48 Joy from the Past

While at a popular coffee shop, I met a former student whom I had taught 13 years earlier. The previous week, I had been thinking about him. He then told me that both he and his sister, whom I also taught, had been speaking of me as well. He gave me a huge, wide, joyful hug!

I recommended a church that he could attend and thanked the Lord for answering my prayer for him. It pleased me that he was happy to see me!

I thank my God upon every remembrance of you, always in every prayer of mine making request for you all with joy.[1]

49 Plugged In at New Levels

When new people get saved today, they seem to grow so fast. They are entering the Body of Christ which has reached new levels of maturity, intimacy with God and revelation of His Word. The Body is reaching and coming closer to its Head, Jesus. These new believers **plug in at a higher place** where none of us were in previous years.

We will speak the truth in love, growing in every way more and more like Christ, who is the head of his body, the church. He makes the whole body fit together perfectly. As each part does its own special work, it helps the other parts grow, so that the whole body is healthy and growing and full of love.[1]

50 Success and Failure

Another person's **success** does not mean my **failure**! Lord, help me to truly and sincerely celebrate another's success! We are encouraged in the Word of God to rejoice with those who are rejoicing.

51 My Fair Lady

I have been reflecting on the magnificent fact that God the Father is preparing a Bride for His Son by the working of the Holy Spirit! The second Book of Corinthians warns us not to be "unequally yoked", that is, not to marry someone who will take us away from God's plans. This Bride that the Father is preparing must become like Jesus, because He will not be "unequally yoked". Therefore, God is transforming us. This process reminds me of the musical, *My Fair Lady*.

It had been years since I had seen the movie. As I viewed it again, I was amazed at the similarities between it and how God is preparing us.

First, Eliza Doolittle was taken from the slums. The Bible relates, that He takes us out of the 'slums' and sits us among the princes.

Before we responded to His love, we were all sinners on our way to hell, which is like living in the slums. The Book of Romans says it this way,

*For **all** have sinned, and come short of the glory of God.*[1]

Back to the movie: then, this slum lady, Eliza Doolittle, was taken in, bathed and put into proper clothes.

Jesus did this for us.
We had to be washed:

*... Christ loved the church and gave himself up for her to make her holy, cleansing her by the **washing with water through the word,** and to present her to himself as a radiant church, without stain or wrinkle or any other blemish, but holy and blameless.*[2]

Our garments had to be changed as well. We see this mentioned in the Book of Isaiah and in the Book of Ephesians respectively.

I shall greatly rejoice in the LORD. My soul will be enthusiastically joyful in my God, for He has clothed me with the garments of deliverance, He has covered me with the robe of acts of loving kindness, like the bridegroom covers himself with ornaments, and like a bride adorns herself with her jewels.[3]

Since Jesus is the Lord of Hosts, the Lord of Heaven's armies, His Bride will also have to be a warrior. She will need armour, which He has so generously provided for her.

*Finally, my brethren, be strong in the Lord and in the power of His might. Put on the **whole armour of God** that you may be able to stand against the wiles of the devil. Stand therefore, having girded your waist with truth, having put on the breastplate of righteousness, and having shod your feet with the preparation of the gospel of peace; above all, taking the shield of faith with which you will be able to quench all the fiery darts of the wicked one. And take the helmet of salvation, and the sword of the Spirit, which is the word of God.*[4]

At last, before Eliza Doolittle was presented to the public she had to have her manner of speech changed. We need to have our manner of speech changed too.

Let your speech always be with grace, seasoned with salt, that you may know how you ought to answer each one. [5]

Our words begin to sound more like something coming out of God's mouth, rather than what used to come out of our own.

Poor Eliza had to keep quoting, "The rain in Spain falls mainly on the plain." We have the privilege and the luxury of quoting God's very own words.

Let the words of my mouth and the meditation of my heart be acceptable in Your sight, O LORD, *my strength and my Redeemer.* [6]

Ultimately, we will become who He wants us to become: a Bride suitable for his Son, Jesus. Have your way in my life Jesus. I want to become Your '**Fair Lady**'!

I must note here that even though there are similarities between God's preparation of the Bride and the musical, "*My Fair Lady*", there are some glaring contrasts. The greatest of these is the arrogance of Professor Henry Higgins. In no way does he resemble our loving Saviour Jesus.

Let him kiss me with the kisses of his mouth. For your love is better than wine. [7]

The voice of my beloved! Behold, he comes leaping upon the mountains, skipping upon the hills. My beloved is like a gazelle or a young stag. Behold, he stands behind our wall; He is looking through the windows, gazing through the lattice. My beloved spoke, and said to me: "Rise up, my love, my fair one, and come away." [8]

Jesus, is loving, kind and so very gentle.

Come to Me, all you who labour and are heavy laden, and I will give you rest. Take My yoke upon you and learn from Me, for I am gentle and lowly in heart, and you will find rest for your souls. For My yoke is easy and My burden is light.[9]

Jesus, I love You and I need your gentle love. Keep changing me more and more into Your image from glory to glory.

But we all, with unveiled face, beholding as in a mirror the glory of the Lord, are being transformed into the same image from glory to glory, just as by the Spirit of the Lord.[10]

52 The Resurrection of the Dead

I believe in resurrected life after death. For truly, life on the other side of death will be much more glorious!

Jesus, when speaking to Martha, told her that He was the resurrection and the life and that if we believed in Him, though we would die, we would live.

If your old self is trying to resurrect itself again, don't believe the lie. Your sins have been done away with by the miracle of His death once and for all. He did not die in vain and you don't have to live in sin." [1]

Amazingly wonderful!

53 The Lamp (The Menorah)

While I was worshipping the Lord with hands upraised, the Holy Spirit said that, in this position, I resembled a **menorah,** or candelabra. The centre branch, my body/spirit receives the oil from God to fill the other branches. My outstretched arms represented its branches.

I asked God to pour His oil from heaven into me that I might be able to be a light to light the nations. This particular word has been given to me prophetically on a several occasions. God's Word says,

> *You are the light of the world. A city that is set on a hill cannot be hidden. Nor do they light a lamp and put it under a basket, but on a lamp stand, and it gives light to all who are in the house. Let your light so shine before men that they may see your good works and glorify your Father in heaven.*[1]

Furthermore, the Holy Spirit reminded me of Jesus when He declared Himself to be the Light of the World.

Lord, duplicate Your light in me by Your grace.

54 His Magnificent Name

I have watched the responses on people's faces when they are respectfully called by name. There is something precious about it. I believe that each of us enjoys hearing the sound of our name.

Jesus is the same! We can't see Him, so we often forget that He is present, or that He does hear us. He wants us to call on Him for the things that we need. When we ask in His name He promises to do it. Jesus' name is all powerful!

> *And whatever you ask in My name, that I will do, that the Father may be glorified in the Son. If you ask anything in My name, I will do it.*[1]

He does love hearing His name, even in a whisper! His name releases a fragrance to change the atmosphere around us.

> *Your name is like its spreading fragrance.*[2]

> *Therefore God also has highly exalted Him and given Him the name which is above every name, that at the name of Jesus every knee should bow, of those in heaven, and of those on*

earth, and of those under the earth, and that every tongue should confess that Jesus Christ is Lord, to the glory of God the Father.[3]

Over the years, I have heard countless stories of people who called on the name of Jesus in their time of peril.

A narrative comes to mind told by a woman. This took place in the 70's. She was praying and calling on the name of Jesus. Suddenly, she had a vision of demons kneeling down and being very angry with her. These demons cried out to Satan to make her stop. Satan's reply: "I can't get up either." Everything in creation has to bow to that name.

55 Where Were You Born?

Here are some possible answers to the question, "Where were you born?"
1. The first or the second time?
2. From above!
3. From God!
4. From heaven!

56 Orchestrated in Heaven

Yesterday, I felt impressed by God's Spirit that when we sing to God, no matter how long or short a song, how talented or not, that heaven not only records it, but also **orchestrates** it gloriously. As well, when we get to heaven we will hear what 'our little song' sounded like!

So sing out my soul! Praise Him and magnify Him for His beauty and His majesty.

O Lord, may Your songs be sung through me!

Sing to the Lord a new song! For He has done marvellous things! [1]

57 Feet and Socks

I was reading and reflecting about Jesus washing the feet of His disciples. He reminded us that we were to humble ourselves and do this to each other. He had given the example.

What joy was mine to recognize that even though I don't wash my husband's or children's feet every week, I do get an opportunity to wash their socks!

58 Testing the Lord

It seemed as though our youngest son Ray was postponing his wedding, so I chose to give that gift-money to charity. To my surprise, he had not postponed the wedding! I wanted to bless him with a generous gift. I felt led to test the Lord as He challenges us in the Book of Malachi. This is the only occurrence in the Bible where the Lord tells us to test Him, and this particular Scripture concerns the giving of finances.

Then, I decided to do what George Mueller used to do regularly: I gave another large gift of money to a charity as a seed-offering and trusted that that seed would produce a large harvest. The world says that this is foolish, but I wanted to operate according to the principles in God's Kingdom. God is My Provider!

I've heard other preachers say, "Give when you can least afford it."

"When you need a miracle: plant a seed."

"Finances prove your spirituality."

"To give is a lifestyle for Christians."

"If you eat your seed there will be no harvest. Seed must be planted."

"Giving is a powerful weapon against the powers of darkness."

"You know that God has your heart when He has your wallet."
Within a very short period of time a large sum of money came to me and I was able to bless Ray and Lyndi with a generous gift. The Lord provided and answered my prayer!

59 Caterpillars and Butterflies

As I was listening to a teaching on the Transfiguration of Jesus and how we are to be transfigured into the glory of God, the Holy Spirit gave me the following parable to understand how this transformation must take place.

But we all, with unveiled face, beholding as in a mirror the glory of the Lord, are being transformed into the same image from glory to glory, just as by the Spirit of the Lord.[1]

In a sense we are all like caterpillars waiting to be changed into butterflies. As the cold weather approaches, caterpillars must choose the cocoon. We must also choose a cocoon of sorts. The fear of winter, darkness, restriction, cold, death, all want us to decide to say, "NO' to winter. Winter usually represents the hard things of life.

However, all caterpillars not in cocoons will die in the winter. So Lord, cause us to embrace the cocoons, for only out of them come butterflies that can soar into the heavens with a brand new beauty, previously unknown to them.

Jesus said that if we would lose our lives for His sake, we would keep them, but if we hung onto our lives we would lose them. That is a word worthy of prolonged consideration.

60 Under our Feet

Every time we do what we are called to do, even when we don't feel like it, we are putting the spirit of death under our feet.

*And the God of peace will crush Satan **under your feet** shortly. The grace of our Lord Jesus Christ be with you. Amen.*[1]

61 Rain On the Just

I was reflecting on this passage,

He makes His sun rise on the evil and on the good, and sends rain on the just and on the unjust.[1]

The Spirit of God was reminding me that when I have read this passage before, or have heard teachings on it, the focus has usually been on the Lord's goodness to rain on the unjust, and that is very true.

Today, He was showing me that it is equally His mercy to let it "**rain on the just**."

What if it rained only on the just for a period of three years? How obvious it would be: our gardens, grass, trees and bushes would be luxurious. The properties of the unjust would be like a desert! It would not take long for the unjust to exercise wrath towards us.

But it has already happened in the past! The prophet Amos tells us that God let is rain on one field and not another; on one town and not on another.

God's rain on the just and the unjust is a form of His protective love for both. He loves us all.

62 A Cloud of Angels and Glory

"Pig Pen" in the Peanuts comic strip always has a cloud of dust over him. Because God's Presence is within me, I believe I walk around with **a cloud of angels and glory** above me. I'm surrounded by a cloud of angels. These angels are continually ascending to heaven and descending to earth, just like those angels on Jacob's ladder.

There was a ladder set up on the earth, and the top of it reached to heaven and, behold, the angels of God were ascending and descending on it.[1]

63 Sun Screen

Yesterday was extremely hot and muggy and today is the same. As I began thinking of all the **sun screen** people will be using, the Spirit reminded me of this passage

The Lord is your keeper; the Lord is your shade at your right hand. The sun shall not strike you by day.[1]

64 Trail Blazer

God has called me to be a **trail blazer**. I sometimes feel as though I have a machete in my hand and I'm clearing the way for a road in the jungle. Progress is slow and difficult. However, after the path has been prepared, others come and quickly build on it. Some will wonder why it took me so long. Others will not ever consider the preparation needed for them to travel on this road. Foundationally, this is the call of the **trail blazer** or the forerunner.

Lord, I embrace Your call on my life. I thank You and praise You because You are the ultimate trail blazer, to the extent that You are even called, "The Way."[1]

Forgive me for not being mindful of all You have done for me. Forgive me for not being mindful or grateful for all those mentors and trail blazers that have prepared a way for me.

I planted, Apollos watered, but God gave the increase. So then neither he who plants is anything, nor he who waters, *but God who gives the increase. Now he who plants and he who waters are one, and each one will receive his own reward according to his own labour, for we are God's fellow workers.*²

I remember the words of Bill Wilson when he spoke at our church, "It's not so much what you accomplish in life, but what you set in motion."

65 The Ark of the Covenant

Just as the Ark of the Covenant represented the Presence of God to Israel, so too, according to God's Word, our bodies are (an ark) the temple of the Holy Spirit. This is not boasting about ourselves, but agreeing with what God has said about us or anyone else who has received Jesus into their hearts.

Just as the Presence of the Lord on the Ark of the Covenant, caused rivers to open up, walls to fall down, victory for God's armies, defeat for His enemies: may God's Presence in me achieve the same results.

Wherever I go, the atmosphere changes and the heavens open up. I have favour with God and man. I am blessed coming in and blessed going out.

*May He be gracious to you and show you His favour.*¹

66 The Storms of Life

As I was driving down the road, the Holy Spirit taught me the following lesson.

We encounter storms in life that could easily overwhelm us. However, there are helpful lessons that will allow us to prevail with success. These were to be learned from Paul's journey to Rome by ship.

*... we came to a place called **Fair Havens...***

Paul advised them, saying, "Men, I perceive that this voyage will end with disaster and much loss, not only of the cargo and ship, but also our lives."...

*So when the ship was caught, and could not head into the wind, we let her drive... And because we were exceedingly tempest-tossed, the next day they lightened the ship. On the third day we **threw the ship's tackle overboard** with our own hands...*

*But after long abstinence from food, then Paul stood in the midst of them and said, "Men, you should have listened to me, and not have sailed from Crete and incurred this disaster and loss. And now I urge you to **take heart,** for there will be no loss of life among you, but only of the ship. For there stood by me this night an angel of the God to whom I belong and whom I serve, saying, 'Do not be afraid, Paul; you must be brought before Caesar; and indeed God has granted you all those who sail with you.' Therefore **take he**art, men, for I believe God that it will be just as it was told me. However, we must run aground on a certain island."*

*Paul said to the centurion and the soldiers, "Unless these men **stay in the ship**, you cannot be saved."*

*And as day was about to dawn, Paul implored them all to take food, saying, "Today is the fourteenth day you have waited and continued without food, and eaten nothing. Therefore I urge you to take nourishment, for this is for your survival, since not a hair will fall from the head of any of you." And when he had said these things, he took bread and **gave thanks to God** in the presence of them all; and when he had broken it he began to eat.*

*And the soldiers' plan was to kill the prisoners, lest any of them should swim away and escape. But the centurion, wanting to save Paul, kept them from their purpose, and commanded that those who could swim should jump overboard first and get to land, and the rest, some on boards and some on parts of the ship. And so it was that **they all escaped safely to land.**[1]*

The key words for coming through the storm are in bold print:
1. Come to a place that will become a **Fair Havens** for you: it might be a quiet room, or a more tranquil time of the day. This is the place for us to be still before God: to trust Him and to worship Him.
2. Begin to **throw excess cargo overboard**: what is the clutter in our lives? It may be possessions, habits, distractions.
   What is it, Lord? We want You to show us!
3. **Take heart!** That is, keep up your courage: this too will pass! We are all subject to similar struggles. These are only a test to see if we will trust in God to bring us through. Then we can give Him the glory. We do not have sufficient strength on our own. Problems are designed specifically so that we have to trust Him or fall apart. Paul's admonition to keep up your courage is mentioned twice in verses 22 and 25. Staying in this attitude requires determination. This only happens 'on purpose'.
4. **Stay in the ship**: no matter how difficult things get, stay with the situation. [Life threatening situations are not included here.] Perseverance will produce endurance.
5. **Give thanks to God**: giving thanks to God produces an attitude of gratitude within us, which is pleasing to God. It takes the focus off our situations and places it where we can be strengthened and refreshed by His Presence.
6. **Everyone reached land safely:** eventually this particular storm in life will pass. We will come through successfully and we will attain new levels of trust in His protection.

67 God and Money

*You cannot serve both God **and** money.*[1]

You can have money, but you can't serve it. I have heard it said that money is a great servant but a cruel master. If people pursued God as diligently as they pursued money, they would have more wisdom in their spending and would learn to sow it for the advancement of His Kingdom

Years ago, while I was reflecting on this very Scripture, the Holy Spirit illuminated something precious to me: every time we are unwilling to serve God, it's usually a matter of money, even though the motive may not be that clear to us! This statement may sound quite judgmental, but God's Word has already spelled it out: God **OR** money! None of this is for judging anyone else except my own heart.

68 Spiritually Pregnant

I was meditating on the one new man: Jew and Gentile, one in Messiah. I had an impression from the Holy Spirit that I was to pray to become spiritually pregnant for this one new man to come forth.

Lord, you have called me to be a 'mother to Israel' and 'a fruitful vine'.

Just before I go off to sleep, I place my hands on my abdomen—the place of the spiritual womb for both men and women. I command life to come forth.

I call forth family members, former students, people I meet on the streets, everyone that I love and all those that I am destined to influence for God's glory. I call forth the Twelve Tribes of Israel by birth order: Reuben, Simeon, Levi, Judah, Dan, Napthali, Gad, Asher, Issachar, Zebulun, Joseph and Benjamin. I call them forth for the fulfillment of their destinies.

69 Faith in the Elevator, the Car and the Chair

The Holy Spirit has been reminding me that sometimes I have more faith in an **elevator** to bring me up higher than I have faith in God. When I press # 9 on the elevator, I am never amazed to be brought to the ninth floor. When I arrive, I never say, "Wow! Can you believe it? I'm at the ninth floor, and all I did was press this button." I realize that I have spent no real energy of my own to get there. I have just exercised faith in the ability of the elevator. As I learn to rest in His Presence, He will bring me up to new levels with Him.

Another example: in my **car**, when it's cold outside I trust the heater to keep me warm. When it's hot I trust the air-conditioner will keep me cool. I trust the windshield wiper to clear a place for me to see when it's raining or snowing. I am never amazed by these performances because I believe that they will function.

Consider a **chair**: when I sit on a chair I believe that it will support me. I never examine it before sitting on it. I trust that it is supportive. I have faith in the chair that it will do what it was made to do.

Help me Lord to put all of my faith and trust in You. You are so superior to anything or anyone else on this planet. Let my vision arise to a higher plane so that I recognize your greatness and rely on You alone. At Christmas time we sing "O come all ye **faithful**, joyful and triumphant..." May this faith be in my heart throughout the whole year.

I declare that You, O God, can bring me to the highest heights!

70 Messenger of the Invisible God

What if you were an invisible parent and you did all the work for your children? You were an invisible sort of servant, and your children didn't know you existed. They didn't know to thank you. You, the invisible parent, would want a faithful messenger to tell the children of your existence and of your labour of love.

That's what I want to be for God: the **messenger of the invisible God**!

How then shall they call on Him in whom they have not believed? And how shall they believe in Him of whom they have not heard? And how shall they hear without a preacher? And how shall they preach unless they are sent? As it is written: "How beautiful are the feet of those who preach the gospel of peace, Who bring glad tidings of good things! [1]

71 A Polished Arrow

The Holy Spirit revealed a process to me concerning the **polished arrow** that is spoken of by Isaiah the prophet.

Here is the process: the first part is to agree with the passage and give the Lord permission to create this polished arrow within my life. Have I considered the probability that I am not yet that polished arrow? What will cause my life to become a polished arrow? What must take place for the Lord to use me as a weapon in His hand? So much self has to be chiselled away!

The Master Carpenter will have to sand the wood before the arrow comes forth. It is impossible to sand from a distance. The abrasive material must, of necessity, rub against the wood, even against the grain. In God's great wisdom He allows close friends, family members and co-workers to become that sand paper. The process is never pleasant, but it is necessary, as the Book of Hebrews makes very clear to us.

Let God train you, for he is doing what any loving father does for his children. Whoever heard of a son who was never corrected? If God doesn't punish you when you need it, as other fathers punish their sons, that it means that you aren't really God's sons at all – that you don't really belong to his family. Since we respect our fathers here on earth, though they punish us, should we not all the more cheerfully submit to

God's training so that we can begin to live! Our earthly fathers trained us for a few brief years, doing the best for us that they knew how, but God's corrections is always right an for our best good, that we may share his holiness.[1]

In that case we surely should be willing to submit to our Father in heaven and endure what He sends to us so that we can live! Once we see the effects of this in our lives, we will rejoice that we had gone through it: wonderful peace will have been produced in our lives.

The arrow may be polished, but it still doesn't have a point. It must now be filed down until almost nothing is left of the wood. Now, very little of self is left. Few allow God to chisel away that much.

O Lord, please make me willing to submit to Your processes, so that Your purposes can come forth on the earth for Your honour and glory.

Jesus calls us to take up our cross daily and follow Him. It will profit us nothing to gain the whole world and suffer the loss of our eternal souls. There is nothing on earth as valuable as a soul!

72 How Odd of God

This is a famous poem. I felt it needed to be a part of this book.
How odd of God to choose the Jews.[1]
But not so odd as those who chose
A Jewish God, but spurn the Jews[2]

73 The Lord's Broken Heart for His People

While reading the 36th chapter of the Book of Ezekiel, beginning with verse 21, I could feel the Lord's heart breaking.
How loving and tender You are, O God of Israel!

But I had concern for My holy name, which the house of Israel had profaned among the nations wherever they went.

"Therefore say to the house of Israel, 'Thus says the Lord GOD: "I do not do this for your sake, O house of Israel, but for My holy name's sake, which you have profaned among the nations wherever you went. And I will sanctify My great name, which has been profaned among the nations, which you have profaned in their midst; and the nations shall know that I am the LORD," says the Lord GOD.

Not for your sake do I do this," says the Lord GOD, "let it be known to you. Be ashamed and confounded for your own ways, O house of Israel!"

Thus says the Lord GOD: "On the day that I cleanse you from all your iniquities, I will also enable you to dwell in the cities, and the ruins shall be rebuilt.

So they will say, 'This land that was desolate has become like the Garden of Eden; and the wasted, desolate, and ruined cities are now fortified and inhabited.' Then the nations which are left all around you shall know that I, the LORD, have rebuilt the ruined places and planted what was desolate. I, the LORD, have spoken it, and I will do it.[1]

*Thus says the Lord GOD... I will increase their men like a flock...**Then they shall know that I am the LORD.**"*[2]

He is totally loving and patient!

74 Repetitions

When a word or an expression is repeated in the Bible it gives it greater significance. The more often it is repeated, the more significant it is.

In the Book of Ezekiel, the expression "*and then they will know that I am the Lord*" is stated **over 60 times**. The repetition of that phrase is astounding. It indicates that it is extremely important to God! At a certain time, God will reveal Himself to the whole world. How blessed we are that we know Him even now! Halleluiah!

75 The Blessing of Proximity

I picked up five pies after the early service this morning that I had previously ordered to support our private school. I gave one pie to my son Ron, because I love him, and he was sitting next to me. My sister and brother in law were visiting that day, and I wanted to bless them, so I gave them a pie. A third pie I gave to member of our congregation who was nearby. Then one of the gentlemen asked me the price of the pies, but I told him that they had to be pre-ordered. Since it was too late for him to do so, I gave him a pie. I brought one pie home. My husband wasn't in the mood for pie, so my mother, who was visiting with us, had a piece, and so did I. A little later in the day, a young bachelor from our congregation came to the house to drop off some papers. He went home with the last half of the pie. It was quite humorous how it all happened!

Then the Holy Spirit reminded me of this: all these people were blessed because they had been physically close to me. I also love the people further away, but only those that were physically close to me got pies. In the same way, God loves every one of us, those close by and those far away, but oh the blessings that come to those who are close by! He is so accessible and He has so much abundance to share with us!

Cause me, O Lord, to develop a greater intimacy with You!
Draw near to God and He will draw near to you.[1]

76 The Door to Another Place

I was watching a commercial on TV last night, and I really don't remember the product or service that was being advertised. Suddenly, a man in the commercial went up to an empty wall, drew a door on it, followed by a door knob and then he turned the knob. He opened the door and entered another place—another country! Wow!

Father God, I choose to draw a door and a door knob on the wall of my life and go wherever You want me to go. I am ready!

Then I said, Here I am! Send me![1]

77 Better Each Time Around

A friend and I were sharing in a restaurant. We said that sometimes it seems as though our lives are going around in circles. While she went to the restroom, the Holy Spirit reminded me that each time we return to the same spot, we have actually returned with increased revelation and a greater depth of character.

It's a bit like a roll of masking tape: each time we complete the circle we add a new layer. The change is ever so imperceptible, yet over a period of time the added layers become obvious.

I am taking the liberty to paraphrase Luke chapter twelve verse two: everything that is hidden, shall be revealed.

78 HPD

Yesterday I was driving behind a UPS truck — United Parcel Service. I felt impressed by the Holy Spirit to declare that I work for

HPD–Heaven's Parcel Delivery. Why this declaration? Because several years prior to this, I had received a prophetic word, "and you will carry gifts and packages that come from Almighty God to you."

79 When I am Weak, Then I am Strong

Over the years I have taken great comfort from the following passage:

And He said to me, "My grace is sufficient for you, for My strength is made perfect in weakness." Therefore most gladly I will rather boast in my infirmities, that the power of Christ may rest upon me... Therefore I take pleasure in infirmities, in reproaches, in needs, in persecutions, in distresses, for Christ's sake. For **when I am weak, then I am strong***.*[1]

These verses have helped me to stay strong through many trials when I was feeling very weak. I have come to realize that God alone is my strength. Over the years, I have come to realize that my weakness is a great asset: it keeps me trusting in Him.

Help me Lord, to realize in every battle that I am not fighting against people, because I do

not wrestle against flesh and blood, but against principalities, against powers, against the rulers of the darkness of this age, against spiritual hosts of wickedness in the heavenly places.[2]

I think the invocation that I use most frequently for calling on God is, "**You are my strength** and my shield."

80 A Prelude to Heaven's Fragrances

The Holy Spirit spoke to me about my new perfume, Chanel # 5. He reminded me that in the Bible, the number 5 stands for grace and He was calling me to be a channel of grace for others.

When I purchased the perfume, I told the young woman that was waiting on me, "Even though this is a lovely fragrance, it is only **a prelude to heaven's fragrances**!"

A garden enclosed is my sister, my spouse... Your plants are an orchard of pomegranates with pleasant fruits, fragrant henna with spikenard...[1]

81 Childhood Dreams

I was about to step into an area where the intercessors were praying during one of our 'Harvest of Glory' Conferences. Then the Holy Spirit reminded me that many of my **childhood dreams** and aspirations were never fulfilled. In my mind, the reason being, 'my father died when I was young'. The Holy Spirit said, "But your Father in Heaven is alive and He is looking out for you. Now all of your dreams and aspirations can be fulfilled!"

He has revealed Himself as a loving father to me. Halleluiah!

82 The Double Portion

While reflecting on the double portion that Joseph, son of Jacob, received, it became obvious to me that the blessing went to his two sons: Manasseh and Ephraim.

I noticed that one of the side-effects of this was that from then on, Joseph's name was rarely mentioned in the Bible. After that, Manasseh and Ephraim's names were mentioned much more frequently.

The revelation was this: the cloak of humility, the willingness to be unseen or unmentioned is needed for the double portion blessing to come forth!

83 Trying to Prove Who We Already Are

During the second temptation of Jesus, Satan said,

If You are the Son of God, You must throw Yourself down."

Jesus didn't have to prove it; He already was the Son of God. This had been confirmed by His Father's voice when Jesus came out of the Jordan River after His baptism,

*"**This is My Beloved Son** with whom I am well pleased.*[2]

Satan did the same thing with Adam and Eve in the Garden of Eden. We read about the same type of temptation in Genesis,

For God knows that in the day you eat of it your eyes will be opened and you will be like God." [3]

But Adam and Eve were already like God! Two chapters earlier in the same book we read,

*So **God created man in His own image**; in the image of God He created him; male and female He created them.*[4]

The devil wants us to try **to prove who we already are**. It is just a trap. The pursuit of the proof is destructive. We must receive and accept by faith who God says that we already are.

84 Praying for God

I have been reflecting for some time now on chapter 14 of the Book of Numbers. It's the place where God plans to destroy the Israelites and start afresh with Moses. When Moses pleads with God not to destroy His people, he is actually praying for the preservation of God's reputation. Moses' intention was that God's reputation would not be tarnished among the nations. In effect, he was **praying for God**!

The Holy Spirit has had me do this too.

In Rick Joyner's book, *The Call*, [1] he describes the three armies of the Lord. The first two are glorious! They are unlike anything this earth has ever seen. But the third army destroys everything accomplished by the first two. There are no lasting tangible fruits for the work of these first two. God receives no glory.

God is calling people out of the third army into the ranks of the more disciplined — those who are submitted to His lordship. The third army will not be tolerated forever. In time, it will disappear. Today is the day to respond to Him.

Now, I am **praying for God** that His glory will be seen on the earth. He is recruiting for the first and second armies. All those in the first two armies were at one time in the third army. They chose to follow Jesus more closely.

Surely, these are words of encouragement.

85 Magnify and Exalt

Jesus! Jesus! Jesus! Jesus! Jesus! This is called **magnifying** His name.

As I **magnify** Jesus, more people are able to see Him in my life. As I empty myself and allow Him to fill me up, He is able to draw many people to Himself.

If I leave His name hidden in my life, not many will see Him. However, the more I **exalt** and lift up His name, He will be seen in me. I must **magnify and exalt Him**.

*Oh, **magnify** the LORD with me, and let us **exalt** His name together.*[1]

86 Thick Black Rope or Fishing Line?

Time after time, the Lord has reminded me that sexual sins, murder, offensive talk, drugs etc. bind people with a **thick black rope.** Their bondage is dark and obvious.

On the other hand, the bondages of religion and self-righteousness are even more binding, but not so visible. These people are tied up with **fishing line** which is transparent, thin, yet extremely strong. They are likewise bound. This fishing line allows them to keep their respectability. Thus, the deception is greater.

Truly I say to you that tax collectors and prostitutes are going into the Kingdom of God before you.[1]

The last 'you' refers to the Pharisees that Jesus was speaking to: the self-righteous ones. He is so wonderfully amazing! The wisdom of Jesus confounds our own!

87 The Power of our Words

We are made in God's image and likeness.

God **spoke** all of creation into being through **the power of His words.** It is also by our words that we speak things into creation: declaring what our children will become, speaking about our situations and circumstances. Am I positive or negative? My words will literally make a world of difference. I need to begin to be more like God who is always calling things into being, even though they don't presently exist.

For example, when I am sick, I need to call forth the healing that was purchased for me on the Cross:

... with His stripes we are healed.[1]

When it is difficult to pay the bills, and if I am tithing, I need to declare that God's is my provider. Then it is helpful to remind ourselves what He told us in the Book of Malachi chapter three.

For every problem or difficulty there is a word or words in the Bible that will give me strength to overcome.

Lord, forgive me for not always declaring my words according to Your plans. I call forth Your purposes for my life and for those that You have entrusted to my care.

88 Canadia?

The Spirit of God was reminding me that those names such as Jerem**iah**, Zechar**iah**, Zedek**iah** all end in "iah". This ending sounds like *yah*. It means *Yah* or *Yahweh* — the Hebrew name for God.

Then He caused me to think of all the countries that have the sound of "yah" at the end of their names, no matter how they are spelled: Austral**ia**, Cambod**ia**, Kore**a**, Ethiop**ia**, Eritre**a**, Alger**ia**, Boliv**ia**, Colomb**ia**, Indones**ia**, Yugoslav**ia**, Malays**ia**, Niger**ia**, Tanzan**ia**, Roman**ia**, Ind**ia** etc. There are at least 40 of them.

Lord, I lift these countries to You. I declare that You are Lord and Master over each and every one of them that bears your name!

O praise the LORD, all ye nations: praise him, all ye people.[1]

Lord, are we Canad**ia**?

89 Fresh Fruit

Yesterday, Bill and I went blueberry picking. We love picking and we both enjoy the fruit. While we were at the farm, the Holy

Spirit reminded me that the blueberry bush does not produce fruit for itself but for others. **Fresh fruit** is best.

Likewise, the fruit in my life produced by the Spirit of God is not for me. It is to feed and nourish others. **Fresh fruit** is best!

In the spiritual realm, we cannot freeze or preserve the fruit produced by the Spirit. **Fresh fruit** is best!

But the fruit of the Spirit is love joy peace, patience kindness goodness, faithfulness gentleness self-control.[1]

90 Buying a Lie?

As the Bible declares,

Jesus said to those Jews who believed Him...

*And you shall know the truth, and **the truth shall make you free.**[1]*

However, the very nature of a lie, no matter how well decorated, will bring the opposite of freedom: pain, disappointment, heart ache and destruction.

The following poem was given to me by the Holy Spirit while doing street ministry in New York City. There, I saw so many lives being destroyed. I wanted them to know the Truth, to be set free, and to enjoy life!

What lie
Did you buy
That makes you
Want to die?

This question needs to be asked each time depressing thoughts come to mind.

91 Recognition

I went to the mall to say good bye to a young man who had been selling Dead Sea products from Israel. His associate had not met me previously, and he thought I was Jewish. I explained to him that I was a Christian and because of that: a spiritual daughter of Abraham.

"Oh" he said, "Of course, the Messiah came and you accepted Him!" He had **recognition** of what it means to be a believer.

92 Happy Birthday # 64

There are meanings attached to numbers in the Bible: number 64= 8x8. Eight has the meaning of new life, or new beginnings. Therefore, 64 is full of new life and new beginnings!

Today, I stand at the threshold of new beginnings.

I receive it! Lord, help me not to hold onto the familiar, the old or the traditional, for You are always making things new.

93 Spiritual Lessons from the Computer

I was reflecting on the complete forgiveness of sins that I have in Jesus Christ. It reminded me of what happens when I press the '**DELETE'** button on the computer.

I thank You, O Lord, You are such a forgiving God.

When I send a document to a friend via the computer, all I have to do is press '**SEND**' or **FORWARD'** and it is on its way. Likewise, when I lift my prayers to God, as soon as I pray He hears me! The whole message that was in my heart arrives swiftly before His throne of grace.

How He loves to hear His children call out to Him. Our prayers are received with gladness.

The beautiful thing about these features on the computer is I can '**SEND**' the same article to many people without losing it. It's like love: when I give it away it only multiplies.

Also I can go to '**SYSTEM RESTORE**' and retrieve a document. That reminds me of God's healing.

I was created in His image and likeness. Sickness and death were never meant to be part of my existence. They entered the world after the fall of Adam and Eve.

However, God loves to restore people to His original plan.

I remember praying for a man who had injured his back. I asked him the date of the accident. He informed me of the date; I touched his back and called out '**SYSTEM RESTORE' in the name of Jesus!** He was healed immediately!

In October of 2011, while in Jerusalem, I met a woman who had been suffering from severe pain in her lungs. Once more, the Holy Spirit reminded me of '**SYSTEM RESTORE**'. I asked her the approximate date of the onset of this sickness. Calling on the name of *Yeshua* I prayed that her lungs would be restored to that earlier date.

A few months later, I spoke to her on the phone and she told me that she had been healed. All the glory to You, *Yeshua!*

I am not advocating a new pattern or a method for healing, but this is how He has led me on a few occasions. *Yeshua* is the Healer and He works through His people by faith. He certainly is the Lord who heals us and He is still doing it today.

The Holy Spirit also '**DOWNLOADS**' more of God into me as I hunger and thirst for more of Him.

He downloads His very life into me by His Holy Spirit.

He downloads more revelation concerning His Word.

He downloads more love into my heart, even for my enemies, because He is the God of love.

If you love Me, keep My commandments. And I will pray the Father, and He will give you another Helper, that He may abide with you forever—the Spirit of truth, whom the world cannot receive, because it neither sees Him nor knows Him; but you know Him, for He dwells with you and will be in you.[1]

He downloads more of His character so that I can reflect the life of Jesus to others.

94 Glorious Beauty

This morning everything was covered with the thickest, most glorious frost that I have ever seen. It covered every branch, every tree, and every weed. The Holy Spirit pointed out to me that only created things were enveloped by the frost. Nothing man-made was covered: signs, fences etc.

The lesson learned: when God's glory comes it will beautify all that has been re-stored by His Holy Spirit. The works of man will remain untouched.

Another lesson: the beauty would not have come unless there had been a heavy fog the night before. At times our visibility is limited, but if we trust through the darkness a new and glorious beauty will appear in the morning.

Weeping may go on all night, but in the morning there is joy.[1]

95 God's Sense of Humour

In 'God My Provider', I shared that God had paid for my last car. Now it was time to purchase a new one; so I did. I trusted Him.

For forty-six months I declared that my car was paid in full. Two months from now, this will be accomplished. My confession will be realized, but not the way I thought it would be. God is my provider and made a way for me to make the payments.

O God, You have a **sense of humour**! You even sit in heaven and laugh!

96 Psalm 104: 30

Recently, I was reminded of a prayer that we used to say in church that is still so important today. It is based on Psalm 104: 30

Come Holy Spirit
Fill the hearts of Your faithful
And enkindle into them
The fire of Your divine love.

Send forth Your Spirit
And they shall be created
And You shall renew
The face of the earth.

97 The Greatest Talent

The Holy Spirit gave me great insight on the parable of the talents, this morning during my devotional time.

Jesus tells a parable about a man going on a journey. Before he leaves, he gives talents to three of his servants, according to the ability of each.

After a lengthy leave, the master comes home to be given the returns on his investments.

The first one, to whom five talents had been given, has invested the money well and he returns an extra five to his master. The one who received two talents also doubled his master's investment.

To both of these, the lord of the house commended them and said told that he was very proud of them.

But the servant, who had only received one talent, thought poorly of his master. His reply indicated that attitude. He told his master that he buried the talent because he was afraid of him. He now returned the original talent with no profit at all.

The master was furious with him. The servant should have at least deposited the talent in the bank to acquire interest.

The Holy Spirit showed me that the greatest gift/talent we have received is the gift of salvation. We need to increase our capacity to share it with others. We want to hear,

Well done, thou good and faithful servant: thou hast been faithful over a few things, I will make thee ruler over many things: enter thou into the joy of thy lord.[1]

Otherwise, if we do not share our salvation with others, along with a tongue-lashing, we will not be able to enter into the Master's joy! Ouch!

O Lord, thank You for this revelation!

98 The Pain of Ingratitude

When we give a gift to someone who feels entitled to it, some of the joy is lost.

How must ingratitude hurt You, Father? You have given so much.

For God so loved the world that He gave His only begotten Son, that whoever believes in Him should not perish but have everlasting life.[1]

Father, I am so grateful for the everlasting life I have received through Jesus. Forgive me when I am presumptuous, ungrateful, and feel entitled.

99 Surrender!

I had just finished a glorious time of worship when I heard the Holy Spirit ask me to surrender the following things in this order:

My Family!

My Friends!
My Finances!
My Future!

I promptly said, "*Hineini.*" [1]

100 Our God is With Us

During our Christmas morning service, as we sang the song, "Emmanuel", I heard the angels singing with us. It was so rich and beautiful; truly it was heavenly.

Emmanuel, our God is with us!
Prince of Peace, Mighty One
The everlasting God.

101 At Home with the Lord

As I reflect on Mom's absence from among us this year, I am reminded of this Scripture:

Now we look forward with confidence to our heavenly bodies, realizing that every moment we spend in these earthly bodies is time spent away from our eternal home in heaven with Jesus.[1]

Though I miss her, I rejoice that my Mom is at **home with the Lord**. I have this confidence that one day I will see her again! At present, she is dancing in His glory!

102 He is My Defense

How many gods are there? Oh multitudes, including the possibility of things like sports, money, homes, looks, intellect, positions, prestige, power, TV, computers etc. It always amazes me that people come to a quick defence of these very things.

As I was reflecting on this, the Holy Spirit said this to me, "They need to defend their gods, but you have the Only true God who is always defending you!" Halleluiah!

He is my defense; *I shall not be moved.*[1]

103 Christ- Messiah

The word Christ comes from the Greek word *Christos,* and means 'The Anointed One'. In Hebrew, the word for anointed one is *Mashiach*, from which we get the word, Messiah. In the late 1980's, the Lord showed me this connection between the two names: Christ and Messiah.

Today through Kenneth Copeland's devotional,[1] I learned that the word Christian means much more than a follower of Christ: it means that I am an anointed one too!

Yes, I am! I am anointed to preach, teach, evangelize, heal, deliver and bring a multitude into the Kingdom of God. Thank You, Messiah *Yeshua,* for your anointing oil from heaven's throne.

104 So I Need You

I've read Anna Roundtree's wonderful book, *The Heavens Were Opened*, several times. [1] I was so blessed by reading it. It inspired me to write the following poem.

I will praise You
As I dance before Your throne

But I would deny You
If I were ever left all on my own.

So I need You
I want You
I desire that You be praised.

Fill my spirit with praise for You!
Fill my heart with songs of love!
Then let the angels ride on this song
As it travels to Your throne above.

Joy! Joy! Joy! Joy!
Angels dancing round!
Joy! Joy! Joy! Joy!
In heaven there is found
Joy! Joy! Joy!

I gather in the many
That I will bring to You
For there aren't any
That can't be embraced by You.

So anoint me for the multitudes
Draw them to Your face
Let them fill the skies above
With praise from every race.

As I keep my face turned towards You
Let oil from heaven fall
Shine on me Your countenance
For I've heard Your glorious call.

105 Hearing God's Voice

At times I have succumbed to the lies of the enemy when he tells me that I am not **hearing the voice of the Holy Spirit**. A sure result of this is I feel beat-up and sad. When I come to my senses, I do know that I have hearing ears because I am one of Jesus' sheep.

My sheep hear My voice.[1]

This morning, the Holy Spirit led me to reflect about the blessings of communion. As a confirmation of my ability to hear the voice of the Holy Spirit, subsequently, two of the three devotionals for that date spoke about communion. Thank you, Holy Spirit, You are the Comforter and You certainly did comfort and encourage me again this morning. How blessed I am! How great You are!

Recently, I have noticed that I hear a little better from the Holy Spirit with a pen in my hand!

106 Auditing or Getting a Credit?

Formerly, when one audited a course at university, it would cost less. Assignments did not have to be completed; consequently, no credit was received.

The same is true of those who come to church just to hear: they are **auditing** the course. They do no assignments and they will get no credit! Hearing only brings deception as James tells us. Hearing only is part of Greek-thought where there is not much room for practical application.

The Greek language focuses on nouns, thoughts and philosophies. Through the ages, this language has come to emphasize levels of position in the church and ecclesiastical hierarchy. When Paul spoke to the Greek Epicureans and Stoics in Athens, they loved to hear him and said that they would talk later. No action followed and no church was ever established there. They were all talk and no action!

Much of the church at large is still operating in the Greek mindset. This has been ongoing since the time of Constantine in the 300's. This type of thinking is contrary to the Hebrew mindset, which is practical and demands an application. The Hebrew mindset is somewhat like the 'NIKE' slogan, "Just do it!" (Of special note: this is nothing against Greek people themselves, but the mindsets that their early philosophers had.)

To get the **credit for taking a course**, we must be willing to pay the full price for what we have heard and it must be applied to our lives. We must do the homework. The Book of James makes it very plain: when we listen only and don't obey we are deceiving ourselves.

I take the liberty to translate this same verse as, "Be not auditors only but take the journey with God for a credit — a heavenly one."

107 Offenses and Deception

During an anointed time of intercession at Antioch Christian Ministries, the Holy Spirit showed me the subtlety of offenses.

If we hang on to them, the enemy puts a thin veil over our eyes. At first, we see rather clearly, but if we continue to stay offended the enemy adds successive veils.

The transformation is gradual and imperceptible, but in time our vision is impaired. We have not become aware that on our side of the veils the enemy has been encoding a new message — a lie. By the time several layers have been added, what we see is the new message which simultaneously has become clearer.

Now we believe the lie to be the truth. This is deception.

108 A Voice-Activated Kingdom

I received an inspiration while meditating on Psalm 27

Hear me when I cry with my voice [1]

Then I began to reflect on atoms and quarks at the sub-atomic level and how they, the quarks, are voice-activated. The Holy Spirit then quickened this to me, "You, O Lord, have **a voice-activated Kingdom!**"

Therefore, I will use my voice to proclaim Your greatness and Your prophetic mysteries. I will declare the magnitude of Your love. I will use my voice to praise Your holy name.

109 Reflections on a Sumac Tree

While my husband, Bill, and I were driving home on a beautiful autumn day, the sumacs along the highway were radiant. Their splendour inspired me to write this poem.

Sometimes life is like a sumac
Neither mighty nor very strong
Growing quite unnoticed
As the seasons move along
But then, in comes the autumn time
And crowns it with a red sublime
Revealing God's own beauty, His wisdom and His power
A sudden burst of beauty in seemingly one hour!
Through the lowly little sumac tree
God is speaking to you and me
Do not seek to be on display
I will reveal you in My own glorious way!

110 The Good Eye

Have you ever wondered about the passages about the 'good eye' and the 'bad eye'? Please read:

Your eye is a lamp that provides light for your body. When your **eye is good**, *your whole body is filled with light.*

But when your **eye is bad**, *your whole body is filled with darkness. And if the light you think you have is actually darkness, how deep that darkness is!* [2]

Alright which one is it? I only have two eyes: is my left eye my good one? Or is it my right eye?

The solution came from the Hebrew language. The good eye and evil eye were common idiomatic expressions in biblical times.

The bad eye, or as some translations have it, the evil eye, refers to someone who is greedy or stingy. I have noticed many Scriptures confirm this. For example:

The Message translation amplifies and opens up the meaning a little more,

Your eye is a lamp, lighting up your whole body... If you live **squinty-eyed in greed**... *your body is a dank cellar.*[3]

Understandably, the good eye is the opposite; it means generous. This generosity is well demonstrated in the Book of Proverbs.

He who has a **generous eye** *will be blessed, for he gives of his bread to the poor.*[4]

What a relief! This is all a matter of the heart!

Keep me generous, Lord, and help me to be kind to the poor for Your name's sake.

111 Forerunner for a Special Season

Our son, Steve had a word of wisdom that blessed me so much and continues to do so. This was it: "We always begin to experience the weather of a coming season before that season starts." For example, we have hot summer-like days before June 21st and we usually experience cold winter-type days before December 21st.

In like manner, I believe that I am one of the **forerunners** for Chapter 14 of the Book of Zechariah which reads,

And it will be that every one that is left of all the nations who came against Jerusalem will go up from year to year to worship the King, the LORD of Hosts, and to keep the Feast of Sukot [Tabernacles].[1]

God in His goodness and mercy has permitted me to experience going up to Jerusalem from year to year to worship the King, the Lord of Hosts, and to keep the Feast of Tabernacles. In going to Israel for the Feast of Tabernacles, I am experiencing the millennial age before it actually fully begins.

Yes Lord, in this I am a **forerunner for a special season**. Soon even greater multitudes will be doing the same thing!

112 Pay Day for Jesus

I have been thinking about this a lot lately: when I go into a store and purchase something, I pay for the item leaving the store with my goods.

However, Jesus paid for our sins. He purchased us with His precious blood.

Therefore take heed to yourselves and to all the flock, among which the Holy Spirit has made you overseers, to shepherd the church of God which He purchased with His own blood.[1]

He didn't get all that He paid for. He paid for the salvation of the whole world, yet this world is still not all saved.

O how patient is our God! But **pay day is coming for Jesus**! Everything that belongs to Him will be His. He paid for us and He deserves to get what He paid for.

113 Wise Men Worship

*Where is He that is born King of the Jews? For we have seen His star in the east and are come **to worship Him**.*[1]

These men had never seen Jesus before, had never heard Him preach nor had seen Him perform a miracle. Yet they came for the specific purpose of worshipping the newborn king of the Jews.

How did they know of Him? How did they know He was a king? How did they know that He was God, to be worshipped? Were there copies of the books of the prophets where they had come from? Were they descendants of those who had a major revival in Persia under Mordecai whose fame is known from the Book of Esther? Was it only the star? There are many questions, but unmistakably, they knew that this child was God and so they came to worship. When I get to heaven I want to ask the wise men how they knew.

We read that Peter got a revelation that Jesus was the Messiah, the Christ, the Anointed One and the Son of God. On this foundation of revelation, Jesus built His church. He told Peter that it was the Spirit of God who gave him that revelation. We read of this account in the Book of Matthew. In essence, this is the same revelation that the wise men had some 30 years prior to this.

The more I ponder about the wise men, the more questions I have. What did they say when they got back home? Did they cause a revival to begin? Were they criticized and persecuted for what they shared?

One thing is sure, their attitude of worship, their willingness to travel a very long distance and the great generosity of their gifts are all powerful examples to me.

Wise men still worship Him today!

114 Three Archangels

The Bible speaks of three archangels: Michael, Gabriel and Lucifer. In Hebrew, *el* at the end of a name means God. For example, Michael means, "who is like God'; Gabriel means "my strength is God". Somehow the name Lucifer just didn't seem to fit in.

From my Latin studies in high school, I remembered that *'luc'* is light and *'fer'* is carrier, making him the carrier of light. Lucifer, in Latin didn't fit at all. His name should also be in Hebrew, and it should end in 'el'. Actually, the Latin language didn't appear until many years after Isaiah the prophet wrote of Lucifer. Somewhere along the line his name had been changed.

I spoke to God about it and entered it into my 'Questions' file on my computer. Within a very short period of time, while reading *The Priestly Bride* by Anna Roundtree, [1]I found Lucifer's name as *Hellel* which means, shining one similar to carrier of light. When I looked up the meaning in Strong's Concordance it is listed as # 1966 which is derived from "from # 1984 in the sense of brightness; the morning star; lucifer." [2]

1984 is the word *'halel'* from which we get the word "Halleluiah". The definition in Strong's Concordance is: "to be clear, originally of sound, but usually of color, to shine, hence, to make a show; to boast and hence to be clamorously foolish... to celebrate...to give light..."[3]

Now it makes sense to me and thank You for revealing it to me so quickly. Now I have it: the **three archangels are Michael, Gabriel and Hellel!**

115 A Parable: The Piano Player

My life is like a piano. Jesus is **The Piano Player**. If He chooses to play a composition with high notes only, He doesn't throw away the rest of the piano! Conversely, if He chooses to play a piece using keys mostly to the left, He doesn't throw away the right side of the piano.

Sometimes in life, He plays those melodies at one end more than the other. I don't understand the tune He's playing. Often these are seasons of difficulties, hard circumstances, defeats, failures, and disappointments.

I do know this: in His good time another song will arise from my life and every key on the piano will be used again for His glory and His pleasure.

You will show me the path of life; in Your presence is fullness of joy.[1]

116 Our God is a Consuming Fire

As we become willing to stay in the Presence of His Consuming Fire, He burns out of us the dross that trips us up on our life's journey. If we are willing to stay put and try not to escape, He will 'fire' our vessel in the kiln of His love. This enables our vessel to contain more of His glory. This fire is not about punishment, judgment or condemnation. It is the refiner's fire of purification.

Today, the Holy Spirit had me pray to be at least willing to allow this to happen. My flesh recoils at the very thought of it. Only by Your enabling grace, O Lord, can this be accomplished within me. It is Your desire, so I place my trust in You.

*Let us have grace, whereby we may serve God acceptably with reverence and godly fear: for our "**God is a consuming fire**".*[1]

117 Another Name

I think that if I could choose another name it would be, Ruth Newman. Here are my reasons.

First, **Ruth** means 'friend'. In the Book of Ruth we see that she, a Moabitess, a Gentile, became a true friend to her mother in law, Naomi, a Jewess. Not only did she befriend her, but through her love, devotion and industry she caused Naomi to come into her lawful inheritance. Besides all of this, Ruth became the ancestor of King David and of Messiah *Yeshua*.

The following passage is often sung at weddings. However, in its original context, the words come from Ruth declaring her dedication to her Jewish mother in law, Naomi.

> *But Ruth said: "Entreat me not to leave you, Or to turn back from following after you; For wherever you go, I will go; And wherever you lodge, I will lodge; Your people shall be my people, And your God, my God. Where you die, I will die, And there will I be buried. The* Lord *do so to me, and more also, If anything but death parts you and me.*[1]

A man named Boaz, who would become Ruth's future husband, took notice of Ruth's integrity and loyalty.

> *And Boaz answered and said to her, "It has been fully reported to me, all that you have done for your mother-in-law since the death of your husband, and how you have left your father and your mother and the land of your birth, and have come to a people whom you did not know before. The* Lord *repay your work, and a full reward be given you by the* Lord *God of Israel, under whose wings you have come for refuge.*[2]

Ruth's influence is further mentioned in the New Testament.

Salmon the father of Boaz, whose mother was Rahab, Boaz the father of Obed, whose mother was Ruth, Obed the father of Jesse, and Jesse the father of King David.[3]

Secondly, the Hebrew meaning of the name **Newman** is 'pleasantness', similar to the meaning of the name Naomi. However, in the English language Newman could be written as 'new-man'.

The cry of my heart is for more Jews and Gentiles to become the one **new man** in Messiah.

Who knows? Maybe one day I'll meet a Ruth Newman, and I'll tell her the meaning of her name!

118 True Air Pollution

While reflecting during prayer this morning, the Holy Spirit told me that negative words are the true air pollution! Jesus said that it was not what goes into our mouths that pollutes, but rather, the words that came out of our mouths.

We need to pay attention to what we say. Words are important and they are living. This is not to condemn anyone but to help us bring more life to our spirit, soul and body. Here are a few quotes to meditate on:

Our **tongue** is the planter of seeds.

*Out of the out of the abundance of the heart the **mouth** speaks.*[1]

Whatever we like the most, hate the most, focus on the most; that is what is going to come out of our mouths.

*If anyone does not stumble in **word**, he is a perfect man, able also to bridle the whole body... Even so the tongue is a little member and boasts great things...*

*See how great a forest a little fire kindles! And the **tongue** is a fire, a world of iniquity. The **tongue** is so set among our members that it defiles the whole body, and sets on fire the course of nature; and it is set on fire by hell... With it we bless our God and Father, and with it we curse men, who have been made in the similitude of God. Out of the same mouth proceed blessing and cursing. My brethren, these things ought not to be so.*[2]

May the words of my mouth and the meditations of my heart be acceptable in Thy sight, O Lord.[3]

We need to say what God's Word declares.
Even Jesus said,

*I only **say** those things that the Father wants me to say.*[4]

*Death and life are in the power of the **tongue**.*[5]

*A wholesome **tongue** is a tree of life.*[6]

*But I say to you that for every idle word men may speak, they will give account of it in the Day of Judgment. For by your **words** you will be justified, and by your **words** you will be condemned*[7]

119 Great Men and Women of God

Speaking of Levi, Scripture says,

For he was still in the loins of his father when Melchizedek met him.[1]

So I asked the Lord, "Who are 'yet in my loins'?"
The Holy Spirit responded, "**Great men and women of God!**"

120 Great Big Angels

In Hebrew and in Greek, the word for angel is *malach* and *angelos* respectively. In both languages it means messenger as well as an angel with wings.

While the TV show 'Touched by an Angel' was popular, I approached a lady on the street to share the love of Jesus with her. She asked if I was an angel, and because I knew the correct definition of *malach* and *angelos*, I answered in the affirmative.

Then she said, "Do me a favour, please. When I turn to go, don't disappear." I assured her that I wouldn't. I had a chuckle on that one and I sensed that heaven was laughing with me.

When I am in Israel, I like to remind soldiers that I ask God to put **great big angels** around them to protect them: *malachim gadolim.*

Today, the Holy Spirit said to me, "Connie, you are one of My *malachim gadolim!*

121 Illumination by Way of a Dream

Can I express this clearly?

Imagine a table top with small figurines on it. Then add a lamp to shine above the little figures. Now introduce pieces of coloured tissue paper and place them between the lamp and the figurines.

The figurines are you and I on the earth and the lamp is Jesus, the Light of the World. The coloured tissue papers are the obstructions that hinder us from getting the full light from the Son. These impediments are principalities from the second heaven. They are part of the culture that we live in.

In my dream, I saw the figurines rising up and poking holes in the tissue paper. This enabled them to receive an unimpeded view of the Light of the World, the Son of God.

Arise, shine for your light has come![1]

122 More of You in My Life

We were singing, "More love! More power! More of You in my life!"

Then the Holy Spirit reminded me that these words were pointless, unless I decided to give Him more of me and more of my time. By doing so, I would be making more room for Him in my life!

> *One thing I have desired of the LORD, that will I seek: that I may dwell in the house of the LORD all the days of my life, to behold the beauty of the LORD, and to inquire in His temple.*[1]

123 The Bread of Life

> *I am **the bread of life**. Your ancestors ate the manna in the wilderness, yet they died. But here is the bread that comes down from heaven, which anyone may eat and not die. I am the living bread that came down from heaven. Whoever eats this bread **will live forever**. This bread is my flesh, which I will give for the life of the world.*[1]

The above statement, made by Jesus, caused many of His followers to leave Him. His Words were profound and full of meaning. These words require reflection and appreciation.

Let us examine a richer implication of what He said.

In the Garden of Eden, God posted cherubim

> *to guard the way to the tree of life.*[2]

God's reason for doing this was,

> *lest he [Adam] put out his hand and **take** also of the tree of life, and **eat**, and **live forever**.*[3]

Notice the highlighted words in the above paragraph taken from the Book of Genesis and those below taken from the Book of Matthew.

*And as they were eating, Jesus took bread, blessed and broke it, and gave it to the disciples and said, "**Take, eat;** this is My body."*[4]

This is the essence of communion: **take, eat and live forever!** The "live forever" part is mentioned by Jesus in John 6, which is in the first paragraph.

When Jesus said, "Take and eat," He was opening the way once again for us to eat from the tree of life: **take and eat and live forever!**

Jesus, You are indeed the tree of life and **the bread of life**.

124 The Work of the Accuser

As I was driving to church I sensed the Holy Spirit say, "As long as you accuse someone, I cannot convict them! Accusing is the work of the enemy. Conviction is My work. Take your choice!"

Lord, have mercy on me and help me to choose You and Your ways only!

*And the great dragon was cast out, that old serpent, called the Devil, and Satan, which deceives the whole world: he was cast out into the earth, and his angels were cast out with him. And I heard a loud voice saying in heaven, now is come salvation, and strength, and the kingdom of our God, and the power of his Christ: for **the accuser of our brethren** is cast down, which **accused** them before our God day and night. And they overcame him by the blood of the Lamb and by the word of their testimony; and they loved not their lives unto the death.*[1]

These verses are self-explanatory.

125 Prayers and Incense

The Holy Spirit helped me to have the following passages come to life from the Book of Revelations.

*Now when He had taken the scroll, the four living creatures and the twenty-four elders fell down before the Lamb, each having a harp, and golden bowls full of **incense, which are the prayers of the saints.***[1]

*Then another angel, having a golden censer, came and stood at the altar. He was given much **incense** that he should offer it with **the prayers of all the saints** upon the golden altar which was before the throne. And the smoke of the incense, with the **prayers of the saints**, ascended before God from the angel's hand.*[2]

This was the illumination: our prayers ascend before the Lord. They are not going into outer space, but they are being gathered as precious incense before the throne of God.

This knowledge has encouraged me to spend more time in prayer, worship and make larger requests of our wonderful God.

As **prayers** ascend to heaven they are as sweet smelling **incense** to God.

126 The Wheat Harvest

It is only those stocks of wheat that are full of plump grain that bend before they are harvested. Those with fewer grains stand erect.

Likewise, the humble whose hearts are full of God bow before Him.

The cry of the Christians during the Welsh Revival was, "Bend me, O Lord."

I say, "Do it again, O God!"

127 How Old Am I Really?

I was wakened in the early hours of the morning with a clarification of the following passages of the Bible. Each one is self-explanatory, but it was the clustering of them together that brought me new depths of understanding.

> Before **I formed you in the womb I knew you;** *before you were born I sanctified you.* [1]

> *Even before **He made the world**, God loved us and chose us in Christ to be holy and without fault in his eyes.*[2]

128 Chosen and Faithful

> *These shall make war with the Lamb, and the Lamb shall overcome them: for he is Lord of lords, and King of kings: and they that are with him are called, **chosen, and faithful**.*[1]

'Chosen' is His part and it's already done!
'Faithful' is our part and it's a work in progress!

129 Fruit

We don't pick fruit from the bark or the trunk of trees. **Fruit** grows on the outer extremities of the smaller branches. This location is most fragile and it's where the fruit can be tossed by storms.

We also have fruit that grows in our lives that can be tossed by storms. Each of us must trust the Lord that this fruit will reach full maturity despite the storms and danger.

When Jesus spoke to storms he said, "Peace, be still." We need to do the same!

130 Parable of the Walnut Trees

Thirty or so years ago, we planted a few Carpathian **walnut trees** in our back yard. The following year, for whatever reason, they had to be moved, and so they were trans-planted. Again, the next year, for whatever reason, they had to be moved and so they were transplanted one more time. The result: they died!

Those who are planted in the House of the Lord will flourish. [1]

The Word says, "Those who are planted" not those who are transplanted. We must learn to stay where God plants us. Through this process of staying put, we learn endurance, we put down roots and we develop maturity.

131 An Unlikely Place

The Bible speaks of something quite remarkable! God invites His people to worship Him in the wilderness.

*Let My people go, that they may hold a **feast** unto me in the **wilderness**.*[1]

In this passage we see that they are called there "to hold a feast". This implies worship, sacrifice and service to Him.

This is not a place of punishment! But it does seem to be **an unlikely place:** one that would never have entered my thoughts. God then reminded me of something Isaiah the prophet said:

For my thoughts are not your thoughts, neither are your ways, my ways.[2]

132 The Pilot Knows

Passengers on an airplane don't have to know how to get that plane airborne. Yet **the pilot knows**.

Parable: as long as we are on board with God, He knows how to raise us up to new levels.

133 Mantles of the Mighty

A mantle is the covering or anointing that is on a person's life. It enables that person to accomplish his destiny. The mantle is needed only while the person is on earth. When an individual departs, his mantle is available to anyone who will pick it up. Elisha picked up the mantle of Elijah as he was taken up into heaven.

Today, in prayer, I asked the Lord for the mantles of several mighty men and women of God.

134 Multiplication

Just as I got out of bed, the Holy Spirit reminded me of Jesus feeding five thousand men, besides women and children.

The crowd had been following Him for three days and Jesus didn't want to send them home hungry. A young boy offered his lunch: five loaves and two small fish. Jesus blessed what had been brought to Him and all were fed. Twelve large baskets of leftovers were gathered after everyone was satisfied.

The revelation was in the **multiplication.** Whatever small thing we bring to Jesus, He can bless it, multiply it and feed a multitude with it.

So I say to You, Lord, "Take my life, bless it, multiply it, and feed a multitude for Your honour and glory.

135 Distillation

Teaching is like the process of the **distillation** of water.
First, you begin with a great amount of material that you know.
Next, you process it through the heat of life's experiences.
Voilà! You have a few drops of clear, clean water to give
to others.

136 In Very Good Company

I was reflecting on the fact that sometimes I love some people
more than they love me. Then, I sensed Jesus say, "I love people
much more than I am loved!"
Thank You, Jesus! I am **in very good company**: Yours!

137 Breakfast with God

Most mornings, I eat breakfast alone.
One morning while doing so the following poem came to mind:
God is strong
God is able
God eats with me at my table!

138 For the Joy That Was Set Before Him

Looking unto Jesus, the author and finisher of our faith, who
for the joy that was set before Him *endured the cross,*
despising the shame, and has sat down at the right hand of
the throne of God.[1]

Can I ever capture the essence of this passage?

*...who for the **JOY** that was set before Him, He endured the cross...*

What was that joy all about? It was about seeing people receive this wonderful gift of salvation.

Jesus, thank You for dying on the cross in my place! It was my sin that deserved punishment, but you took upon Yourself the punishment for all of the sin of the world.

Yet it pleased the LORD to bruise Him; He has put Him to grief. When You make His soul an offering for sin... He shall see the labor of His soul, and be satisfied. By His knowledge My righteous Servant shall justify many, for He shall bear their iniquities... Because He poured out His soul unto death, and He was numbered with the transgressors, and He bore the sin of many, and made intercession for the transgressors.[2]

The words to the following song by E. J. Crum help make this point quite clear.

He paid a debt He did not owe
I owed a debt I could not pay
I needed someone to wash my sins away
And, now, I sing a brand new song
"Amazing Grace."
Christ Jesus paid a debt that I could never pay. [3]

139 My Holy Mountain

*Great is the LORD, and greatly to be praised in the city of our God in **His holy mountain**. Beautiful in elevation, the joy of the whole earth, is Mount Zion on the sides of the north, the city of the great King.*[1]

*They shall not hurt nor destroy in all **My holy mountain**.*[2]

*Even them I will bring to **My holy mountain**, and make them joyful in My house of prayer...*[3]

*... But he who puts his trust in Me shall possess the land, And shall inherit **My holy mountain**.*[4]

*For on My **holy mountain**, on the **mountain** height of Israel," says the Lord GOD, "there all the house of Israel, all of them in the land, shall serve Me; there I will accept them...*[5]

*O Lord, according to all Your righteousness, I pray, let Your anger and Your fury be turned away from Your city Jerusalem, **Your holy mountain**...*[6]

*Blow the trumpet in Zion, and sound an alarm in **My holy mountain**!*[7]

*I am returned unto Zion, and will dwell in the midst of Jerusalem: and Jerusalem shall be called a city of truth; and the mountain of the LORD of hosts, the **holy mountain**.*[8]

Why so many quotes? I want to establish what God has already spoken: **His mountain is holy**! And now, this is the revelation that I received.

In Hebrew, the letter that most signifies holiness is the letter 'shin' which is shaped like a rounded off 'w'. There are three valleys that carve out that holy mountain in Jerusalem: the *Kidron* Valley, the Tyropoeon Valley and the Valley of *Ben-Hinon*. These are carved out in such a way that they form the letter 'shin'.

When God calls His mountain holy, He put His literal stamp on it!

140 Fresh Bread

May the fragrance of the fresh bread from God's Presence draw us into His kitchen!

Jesus told us that He was the bread of life. If we would come to Him, we would never hunger.

141 How to Spell Israel

The spelling of the word Israel in Hebrew is quite unique and amazing!

The first letter is the letter *'yud'*. It is the smallest letter of the Hebrew *'alef bet'*. It is written like an apostrophe. The last letter of the word Israel is *'lamed'*. It is the tallest letter in the Hebrew *'alef-bet'*.

There is a powerful lesson here: like Israel, we may begin small, but in God's eyes we can finish with greatness.

*Then the LORD your God will bring you to the land which your fathers possessed and you shall possess it. He will **prosper you and multiply you more than** your fathers.*[1]

142 Prayer in the Parking Lot

I was shopping at Costco, and a young worker came to me and said, "I don't remember your name, but I remember your son Steve's. You both prayed for me in this parking lot last summer. My wife had been unable to conceive and guess what? We're expecting in a few months! We're soooooooo happy! Thank you, again."

Sing, O barren, you who have not borne! Break forth into singing, and cry aloud, you who have not laboured with child! [1]

The beauty of prayer is: God does it all; we just make ourselves available.

143 Song: "O Israel"

One afternoon I had spent a short time in intercession for Israel. I picked up my pen and this song came from my spirit. It was effortless! The melody for it is the national anthem of Canada. This blessed me in a particular way because I felt that through this song, God was connecting Canada and Israel for His purposes.

O Israel
Your land is surely blessed
It has been given
As a place where you should rest
But the wars do rage
Throughout history's page
And peace far from your walls
But your God is great to deliver
When to Him you do call
We bless God's name
We stand with you
O Israel, we stand on guard for thee
O Israel we stand on guard for thee.[1]

144 Follower of Christ/Messiah

I received a very encouraging phone call from a friend. She blessed me with these words:

"When I am indecisive I ask myself, "What would Connie do?"" When Paul the apostle was speaking he said,

Therefore I urge you, imitate me. For this reason I have sent Timothy to you, who is my beloved and faithful son in the Lord, who will remind you of my ways in Christ.[1]

I do not share this to puff myself up. It has been a prayer of mine for many years that others would follow me as I **follow Christ the Messiah**.

145 The Lands of Zebulun and Napthali

Matthew chapter four:

The land of Zebulun and the land of Naphtali, by the way of the sea, beyond the Jordan, Galilee of the Gentiles: the people who sat in darkness have seen a great light, and upon those who sat in the region and shadow of death light has dawned.[1]

Both of Jacob's sons **Zebulun and Napthali** received prophetic words when they were younger.
From the Book of Judges we read

*...out of Zebulun they that handle the **pen of the writer**.[2]*

The Book of Genesis tells us,

*Napthali is a hind let loose: he **gives goodly words** (delivering words of beauty).[3]*

Jesus spent almost 30 years in the region of Zebulun and Napthali and He is the Light that has dawned. He is also the "***goodly word***": His words are the beautiful words of the Good News. When the "***pen of the writer***" copied these words, they became known as the Gospels.
All of this came from **the lands of Zebulun and Napthali.**

146 Obedience

I was reflecting on the word obedience, and I knew it had Latin origins.

The Holy Spirit highlighted the word *Obed* in <u>obed</u>ience. *Obed* is a Hebrew name and it means to serve.

The meaning of obedience has just been expanded for me: **obedience** means service to God and others.

147 Prophetic Gestures

The first time I saw someone use an I-Pod screen I was quite impressed. I saw hand motions that enlarged and diminished pictures, and I sensed they could be powerful **prophetic gestures**.

I began using these gestures while praying and making declarations.

In the enlargement mode I declared:

"Salvation is being increased across our nation."

"Fruitfulness breaks forth to the surrounding farmlands."

"Peace is being enlarged in schools for teachers and students."

In the diminishing mode I declared:

"Sin, you are losing your power over this nation."

"Sickness is not a part of this region anymore."

"And the inhabitants will not say, I am sick." [1]

It will be exciting on the other side to see the full effects of these prophetic gestures accompanied by my declarations of faith.

148 Jesus, the Lamb of God

While reflecting on Jesus' sacrifice as the Lamb of God, I recognized that He took upon Himself our sin **and sicknesses**.

As a result, we can walk in the perfection of divine health.

*For the law of the Spirit of life in Christ Jesus has made me free from the law of sin and **death**.*[1]

Sickness often leads to death. We have been set free!

149 God's Glory

Fresh fallen snow can transform the landscape into a place of beauty and majesty.

However, we must be careful not to allow this splendour to lose its wonder.

How much more will **God's glory** transform the earth? We have seen snow, but we have not yet seen our land blanketed with His glory.

Come, Lord Jesus, come! Come in majesty and glory! Transform and beautify!

I've heard part of the Lord's Prayer translated, "As it is in heaven, yes, on earth."

150 Beauty for Ashes

I was reflecting on Isaiah's passage *"to give unto them beauty for ashes."*[1] The Holy Spirit reminded me of a prophetic word that our Woodslee Prayer Community Church had received several years ago: "We would be the wood for the revival fires."

When wood burns it produces ashes. Our church now needs to expect to be beautified by the Lord because He gives *"**beauty for ashes**."*

151 Sacrificing to Idols

I heard this word inside of me, "Don't **sacrifice to idols**: it will only bring you grief." And then these definitions came to me.

Idols: anything or anyone that keeps me from God or takes first place in my life other than God.

Sacrifice: to give idols my time or talent or money or energy or strength or skills or virtue and beliefs.

Grief: disappointment that there is no pay day; no rewards; emptiness; sadness; anger; possible bitterness and unforgiveness; lack of fruit; aloneness and isolation.

152 Now I Know Why

In the early spring of 2009, the Holy Spirit told me that my trip to Israel for 2010 would be in November—not in September as other years.

I am usually there for the Fall Feasts: Trumpets/*Yom Teruah*, the Day of Atonement/*Yom Kippur* and Tabernacles or *Sukot*. In November, there would be no feasts. However, I had great peace knowing that my instruction was from the Lord. Father knows best!

During 2010, I incurred the greatest debt of my life. My November's trip appeared to be an impossibility.

However, I continually declared that I would be going to Israel in November contrary to my circumstances. When people inquired, I replied I knew that God would provide. I never doubted, not even once!

Jesus taught us that we can have whatever we say. We can speak to mountains and say, "Move!" and they will! The condition is we have to believe and not doubt. This ingredient of faith is vital for answered prayer.

Sure enough, a month before I left, someone gave me air miles for my flight. My wonderful and generous children gave me another large birthday party. My birthday is at the end of October! Most people gave gifts of money. Lo, and behold, I had the required finances to go and to bless others in the land.

It took me three years to realize why God told me that I would be going in November. He knew I had no money till then, and He knew that my children would be giving me a party.

Now I know why! I was a little slow I admit, but finally I got it!
The obscure, we see.
The obvious, takes longer!

153 An Encouraging Picture

My weekend was a very difficult one. Satan had been sending his darts of discouragement and hopelessness.

The cry of my heart was, "My trust and hope are in You alone, O Lord. Let faith arise! Let Your love abound toward me and through me."

Then I looked out the window and caught sight of a majestic snowfall. Even the tiniest tree branches had ten centimetres of clean, fluffy snow. There wasn't a breeze. It was a picture of loveliness!

I believe, O Lord, it was a small example of the transformation that takes place in the soul of one who trusts in You—one who refuses to listen to the lies of the enemy.

Thank You for this **encouraging picture!**

154 From a Message that I Heard

I heard this message many years ago. I believe the poetic form of the four key words captured my thoughts so well that the preacher's message comes to me frequently. He said that there were four things to hinder our walk with God:

1　**Vows:** those that are made under pressure or ungodly ones.
2.　**Wows:** looking for the fantastic instead of following the Word.

In John six we read about the miracle of Jesus multiplying the bread and feeding five thousand men: **Wow!** In the same chapter,

Jesus revealed Himself as the Bread of Life. After doing so, all but His disciples left Him. We must remember the Word, not the wow!

3. **Woos**: things that **woo** us way from God. Lot's wife is an example. She was enticed by Sodom and it brought about her destruction.
4. **Woes**: all of the anguish and unpleasant events that wound our hearts.

155 God's Pity on our Clocks

Each Biblical number has a special meaning. In the Book of Revelation, the number six is related to man and the beast.

Wisdom is needed here. Let the one with understanding solve the meaning of the number of the beast, for it is the number of a man. His number is 666.[1]

In God's foreknowledge, our clocks can never read 6:66.
The largest number capable of repeating itself three times on a clock is 5, as in 5: 55.
Five is the Biblical number for **grace**. Repeated three times it becomes noteworthy of His outstanding Grace! Grace! Grace*!*

*For the Lord God is a sun and shield: the Lord will give **grace** and glory: no good thing will he withhold from them that walk uprightly.*[2]

*And of his fullness have all we received, and **grace** for **grace**.*[3]

Let me not wait until 5: 55 a.m. or p.m. to thank You, O God, for Your kindness and **pity on our clocks!**

156 'Spider Man Like' Activity

I had a vision of something during a morning of outstanding intercession. This occurred when I called on the name of Jesus. There appeared to be **'Spider Man like' activity**. I saw white strings of substance that would emanate from God's hands. These white strings would connect heaven with the people as I prayed for them!

And whatever you ask in My name, that I will do, that the Father may be glorified in the Son. If you ask anything in My name, I will do it.[1]

157 Spare Time

This question came to my mind one day, "What do I do in my spare time?"

I believe that the Holy Spirit said this to me, "Through prayer, you are changing the world!"

We're told in God's Word, the sincere prayer of a righteous person is very effective and produces glorious results.

158 Aaron's Staff

As I woke up one morning, the following passage from the Book of Numbers came to mind.

Now it came to pass on the next day that Moses went into the tabernacle of witness, and behold, the rod of Aaron, of the house of Levi, had sprouted and put forth buds, had produced blossoms and yielded ripe almonds![1]

Aaron's staff produced vegetation: sprouts, buds, blossoms and ripe fruit. This is a picture of the Garden of Eden before the fall. Everything in the Garden was constantly producing life.

A parable for our lives:

We have been redeemed by the precious blood of *Yeshua*. We have been restored to life!

> *For the law of the Spirit of life in Christ Jesus hath [has] made me free from the law of sin and death.*[2]

Now, our lives are simultaneously bearing sprouts, budding, blossoming and producing mature fruit for God's glory!

The more we abide in Christ Jesus; the more our lives abound with fruit.

159 A Prayer for Trust in God's Provision

Lord, please help me to trust You more as my great Provider!

I have been acting foolishly: a soldier does not save to buy his own gun or tank because the army provides once enlisted!

Lord, I have enlisted in Your army, and I know that You provide for me

> *The LORD will perfect that which concerns me; You mercy O LORD, endures forever; Do not forsake the works of Your hands.*[1]

160 The Price of Gas

Today, the sign at the gas station read $1.29.9. This is in Canadian dollars and it is per litre not per gallon. [Conversion: 1 USA gallon = 3.78 litres: $4.91/gallon]

As I was filling up the price at the pump was $1.22.6!

On my way home later in the day, many places had the price of gas listed as $1.34.9

Thank you, Lord, for protecting my finances.

*But seek ye first the kingdom of God and his righteousness; and **all these things** shall be added unto you.*[1]

161 Covenants

The Lord had been reminding me of the **covenants** that He made to me personally: that He would anoint me to bring a multitude into His Kingdom and that my eyes would see it!

During the Christmas holidays I was given a book to read. In it, the author referred to **covenants** quite frequently. Also a publication arrived, early January. The topic was 'The Four **Covenants**' made with: Abraham, Moses, David and the New **Covenant** made in the Blood of Jesus. Following that, my friend taught on the **covenants** including the one with Adam. Again in the same month, Mom loaned me a book about '**Covenant** House' in Toronto.

I thank you Lord that you are speaking to me about **covenants.** I rejoice that you are faithful to every one of Yours!

I have made a covenant with My chosen.[1]

162 A Trauma Unit

I woke up with this deep sense that other Christians and I needed to become a type of trauma nurses and doctors and activate a **trauma unit.**

There are many people who have experienced emotional trauma. They are stuck there often alone and quite helpless. The trauma often results in physical sickness and emotional battles, depressions, and sorry to say, even suicide. When help is available, healing and change are the positive results. Without the help these wounded ones become ineffective in advancing the Kingdom of God here on earth: their pain is too great for them to appreciate anything beyond themselves.

Lord, show us how to come alongside those who need a friend. Help us to stand with them until they can come through. Help us to help them put their trust in You, because You are faithful to your Word.

I will never leave you nor forsake you." So we may boldly say: "The Lord *is my helper; I will not fear. What can man do to me?* [1]

163 Make your Breathing Count

Often when I inhale, I declare, "I am breathing in the atmosphere of heaven."

When I exhale, I declare, "I am releasing the atmosphere of heaven onto earth."

Let everything that has breath praise the Lord.[1]

164 Making Sweet Music

I was reflecting on the fact that we often have very different points of view, even from our friends. Yet, God has brought us together in this world to make a beautiful sound for Him. I wasn't sure just what that sound was- not classical, maybe a bit contemporary, often syncopated, but music to the Lord. Fifteen minutes later, I was reading in Graham Cooke's book, "*A Divine Confrontation*"[1], where he said that many opposite points of view often will remain opposite, but that people can still work together. He called it a type of harmony.

The *Webster's Dictionary* defines harmony as 'a pleasing agreement of parts, color, size etc." [2] So, by definition, harmony can only take place because there are differences. We can be different but we can run parallel to each other, and work for common goals. Harmony is true in music as well as in relationships.

There it was in black and white right in Graham Cooke's book! Thank you Lord! That's it: we are harmonizing and that is surely **making sweet music!**

Sing unto the Lord a new song![3]

165 Parable of the Filling Station

To be able to fill my car with gas I have to get out of the traffic, drive into a filling station, turn off my engine and open the 'receiver'- the door to the gas tank.

The same is true to get filled with more of God's Presence:

I must get out of the rush of life and get into a quiet place alone, turn off my own thoughts from the distractions of life and open myself to receive more of Jesus.

> *One thing I have desired of the LORD, that will I seek: that I may dwell in the house of the LORD all the days of my life, to behold the beauty of the LORD, and to inquire in His temple. For in the time of trouble He shall hide me in His pavilion; in the secret place of His tabernacle He shall hide me; He shall set me high upon a rock.*[1]

166 A Vision of Sifting

I had just left the Clal building in Jerusalem. While I was walking down the steps, I had a **vision of a great sifting** that was going on.

It was as if people were peas on a giant conveyor belt and they didn't realize it, but they were being sorted.

God showed me that people think that everything is going on the same as usual. While the outward appearances may indicate this, a major separation of people is taking place in the spirit. In time it will be visible in the natural realm.

When the Son of Man comes in His glory, and all the holy angels with Him, then He will sit on the throne of His glory. All the nations will be gathered before Him, and He will separate them one from another, as a shepherd divides his sheep from the goats. And He will set the sheep on His right hand, but the goats on the left. Then the King will say to those on His right hand, 'Come, you blessed of My Father, inherit the kingdom prepared for you from the foundation of the world.[1]

Keep me close to You, O Lord!

167 God's Son

We were out for street ministry today. It was unseasonably beautiful: a warm, bright, sunny, January day! Everyone appeared to be enjoying this rare happening! The sun was influencing all of us; giving us a sense of well-being; and beckoning people to come outside. During our winter days that are very cold, many people tend to stay indoors.

A parallel: How much more beautiful, welcoming, beckoning, comforting, influencing, radiating is the Son of God!!! Shine through us Jesus.

Let us feel the warmth of Your Presence!

The Holy Spirit reminded me that the sun is a star in our solar system. **God's Son**, on the other hand, is the Creator of all the stars as well as the rest of the universe.

For the LORD God is a sun and shield; The LORD will give grace and glory; No good thing will He withhold from those who walk uprightly.[1]

...and having in his right hand seven stars; and out of his mouth a sharp two-edged sword going forth; and his countenance as the sun shines in its power.[2]

May we radiate the warmth of the **God's Son** to those who don't know **Him** yet!

168 The Cherubim and Seraphim

This morning during a very powerful time of intercession at Antioch Christian Ministries, as we were worshipping, the Holy Spirit reminded me that the **cherubim** were guardians of God's glory and the **seraphim**, the burning ones, were present when God's glory was revealed to the prophet Isaiah.
We see this in the following passages:

*So He drove out the man; and He placed **cherubim** at the east of the Garden of Eden, and a flaming sword which turned every way, **to guard** the way to the tree of life.*[1]

*and behind the second veil, the part of the tabernacle which is called the Holiest of All, which had the golden censer and the ark of the covenant overlaid on all sides with gold... and the tablets of the covenant; and above it were the **cherubim** of glory overshadowing the mercy seat.*[2]

*I saw the Lord sitting on a throne, high and lifted up, and the train of His robe filled the temple. Above it stood **seraphim;** each one had six wings: with two he covered his face, with two he covered his feet, and with two he flew. And one cried to another and said, "Holy, holy, holy is the Lord of hosts; the whole earth is full of His glory!"*[3]

The word **Cherubim**, is the Hebrew plural form of the word *chereb,* meaning sword. These beings were guardians. They protected the way of the tree of life. Present also was that flaming revolving sword. And over the mercy where God's glory appeared, the **cherubim** were positioned as guardians of His glory.

The word **Seraphim,** is the Hebrew plural form of the word *seraph* meaning the burning ones. These were in the throne of God.

This was the inspiration:

We are carriers of His Presence, and His glory accompanies His Presence. Therefore, we need **cherubim** all around us to guard the glory of His Presence within us!

The Book of Hebrews states, *"For our God is a consuming fire."* [4]...So we need the **seraphim** who are the burning ones, to be with us too.

169 Arise, Shine

During prayer time, I was reflecting on the very correct order of the first two words in Isaiah 60:

Arise, shine.

The passage doesn't say, "Shine and arise" because we must arise from our slumber, our apathy, our selfishness before we can shine.

The shine of His glory is outflow of arising.

The whole first two verses of Isaiah 60 are simply beautiful.

Arise, shine; for your light has come! And the glory of the LORD is risen upon you. For behold, the darkness shall cover the earth, and deep darkness the people; but the LORD will arise over you, and His glory will be seen upon you. [1]

God, Your Word is so perfect: even the order of the words themselves have a message there for us! Thank You!

170 Declaration Fulfilled

In 2006 I read Bill Johnson's book, *When Heaven Invades Earth.*[1] I was so captivated by what I read that I began declaring, "One day, I am going to Bethel Church in Redding California. I will be in his church."

It took 6 years, but I always kept the declaration fresh in my mind.

Now I've been twice: once in 2012 and again in 2013.

*For assuredly, I say to you, whoever **says** to this mountain, 'Be removed and be cast into the sea,' and does not doubt in his heart, but believes that those things he **says** will be done, he will have whatever he says.*[2]

God tells us in His Word that we can have what we say, but we usually just keep saying what we have. I believe that words are the most powerful force in the universe!

171 Huge DNA

While on my way to the nearby city, the sky was exceedingly clear. I was to meet the Police Chief and present him with a gift of gratitude from our street ministry group, along with one of our pastors.

Suddenly a cirrus cloud formed in the sky shaped like a perfectly formed **huge DNA** coil. It stayed in that position for at least twenty minutes. I wished I had my camera with me!

I sensed that the Holy Spirit was saying that through our divinely orchestrated appointment with the Chief that the DNA over the city had changed.

Therefore I exhort first of all that supplications, prayers, intercessions, and giving of thanks be made for all men, for kings and **all who are in authority**, *that we may lead a quiet and peaceable life in all godliness and reverence.*[1]

172 Possess Your Possessions

Possess your Possessions[1]

I read this passage many times while studying the Book of Obadiah, but I never paid much attention to it until I received a few prophetic words about possessing my possessions.

Then the Holy Spirit reminded me that I also have an inheritance to possess. What is it Lord?

I know some of what it is, but I will have to reflect on this some more.

For sure **the Lord** is my inheritance. The Lord is my portion

The LORD is the portion of my inheritance. [2]

Certainly, my **children** are my inheritance:

Behold, children are a heritage from the LORD.[3]

Also, a part of my inheritance is the **multitude of souls** that I want to bring into God's kingdom for His honour and glory.

The fruit of the righteous is a tree of life, and he who wins souls is wise.[4]

I also anticipate that everything that I do will prosper,

Blessed is the man who walks not in the counsel of the ungodly, nor stands in the path of sinners, nor sits in the seat of the scornful; but his delight is in the law of the LORD, and in His law he meditates day and night. He shall be like a tree planted by the rivers of water that brings forth its fruit in its season, whose leaf also shall not wither; and **whatever he does shall prosper.**[5]

Furthermore, my **family, friends, acquaintances**, co workers, former students, people that I've met on the streets of the cities, and towns, as well as all those that I will meet in the future. I believe that there are no accidents regarding the people that we meet in life. I desire that each one will spend eternity in heaven with God.

For I know the plans I have for you, says the LORD. *They are plans for good and not for evil, to give you a future and a hope.*[6]

Good health is another thing that God wants me to seize.
Why would the Father have allowed His Only-Begotten Son Jesus to suffer and die for our sins and sicknesses if He didn't want us to be well? The Word of God is full of His promises to keep us well. Her are just a few examples:

I am the LORD *who heals you.*[7]

And the inhabitant shall not say, "I am sick"[8]

But He was wounded for our transgressions, He was bruised for our iniquities; The chastisement for our peace was upon Him, and **by His stripes we are healed.**[9]

For I will restore health to you, and **heal you** *of your wounds,' says the* LORD*."* [10]
Of course, the classic example of healing is found in the life and ministry of Jesus.

How God anointed Jesus of Nazareth with the Holy Spirit and with power, who went about doing good and **healing all** *who were oppressed by the devil, for God was with Him.*[11]

Here I want to add a special note that confirmed my belief that God wants to heal us.

Paul, our oldest son, who was nineteen at the time, was in a life-threatening motor cycle accident. Because I was convinced of God's will for him to be healed, I and many others began to declare that God was going to heal him. The prophetic word that accompanied this was, "What the doctors cannot do: God will do." We watched God perform a miracle that would otherwise not have taken place, had many of us not prayed with the conviction that God was able to do it. I give Him all the glory for saving our son's life.

A legacy of a **long life** is also my inheritance. More and more, I recognize how few people know that there is a promise attached to the commandment to honour our fathers and mothers. This is the promise: a long good life! If a long, good life is a reward, then I choose to possess a long life.

*The righteous shall flourish like a palm tree. He shall grow like a cedar in Lebanon. Those who are planted in the house of the Lord shall flourish in the courts of our God. They shall still bear fruit in **old age**; they shall be fresh and flourishing.*[12]

This promise alone beats all of the beauty creams that promise rejuvenation!

Actually, there isn't a promise in God's Word that I cannot appropriate because

All the promises *of God in Him are Yes, and in Him Amen, to the glory of God through us.*[13]

So I will continue to read the Word, so I will continue to pray, so I will continue to declare, so I will continue to appropriate God's promises until I **posses all of my possessions**!

With God there is such abundance!

173 Enough Jurisdiction

While I was shopping at the supermarket in town, I saw the new butcher and addressed him with, "God bless you!" His reply rather startled me, "Well, I would bless you too, but I don't know if I have **enough jurisdiction** to do that!"

We who have been born-again, not only have the privilege of blessing others, but it is our responsibility, to let them know that God loves them. In Peter's first epistle he tells us that we are as believers are *"a chosen generation, a royal priesthood."* [1]

Under the Old Covenant, the priesthood tribe was that of Levi. Part of their duty as priests was to minister to God and to pronounce blessings in the name of the Lord.

As New Covenant believers, we have the jurisdiction to minister to God also and bless others.

Could we start an 'epidemic' of blessing each other? What can be better than the blessing of the Lord?

The blessing of the Lord *makes one rich, and He adds no sorrow with it.* [2]

174 Keys of the Kingdom

*And I will give you the **keys of the Kingdom** of Heaven. Whatever you forbid on earth will be forbidden in heaven, and whatever you permit on earth will be permitted in heaven.* [1]

Keys are for opening and closing doors. Jesus has given us the keys to His Kingdom. Therefore, I choose and declare, along with many praying friends, that we will close the doors to whatever would keep the Hebrew people in *diaspora* and we will open the doors to *aliyah*.

Diaspora refers to all of those Hebrew people leaving outside of the modern state of Israel. *Aliyah* is a Hebrew word that literally means to arise, but it is used also to denote that Hebrew people are returning to Israel, their homeland.

We pray this with such confidence knowing that we are aligning our prayers with the Word of God. There are easily a hundred and fifty or more references in the Bible about the Jews returning to Israel at this time in history. Here are a few of them:

> *The LORD your God will bring you back from captivity, and have compassion on you, and gather you again from all the nations where the LORD your God has scattered you. If any of you are driven out to the farthest parts under heaven, from there the LORD your God will gather you, and from there He will bring you.[2]*

> *Fear not, for I am with you; I will bring your descendants from the east, and gather you from the west; I will say to the north, 'Give them up!' and to the south, 'Do not keep them back!' Bring My sons from afar, and My daughters from the ends of the earth.[3]*

> *But I will gather the remnant of My flock out of all countries where I have driven them, and bring them back to their folds; and they shall be fruitful and increase.[4]*

> *Therefore thus says the Lord GOD: 'Now I will bring back the captives of Jacob, and have mercy on the whole house of Israel; and I will be jealous for My holy name, then they shall know that I am the LORD their God, who sent them into captivity among the nations, but also brought them back to their land, and left none of them captive any longer.[5]*

> *At that time I will bring you back, even at the time I gather you; for I will give you fame and praise among all the peoples*

of the earth, when I return your captives before your eyes,"
says the L*ORD!*[6]

Thus says the L*ORD of hosts: 'Behold, I will save My people*
from the land of the east and from the land of the west; I
will bring them back, and they shall dwell in the midst of
Jerusalem. They shall be My people and I will be their God,
in truth and righteousness.[7]

175 Sources of Production

This sounds very simple but yet it is profound:

Bakeries produce donuts.
Canning factories produce canned food.
Sin-nature produces sin.

If we want to get rid of donuts, canned food and sin, we will
have to eliminate the sources of production: bakeries, canning
factories and sin nature. We really don't want to eliminate donuts
and canned food.

Jesus didn't just forgive our sins, but He eliminated the sin
nature when He died on the Cross and rose from the dead. He
destroyed the sin nature for us and did it in our place.

Our privilege has been to receive this wonderful gift of
salvation.

There was nothing that we could have done to earn such a
gift. It was free!

For the wages of sin is death; but the gift of God is eternal life
through Jesus Christ our Lord.[1]

For Christ did not enter into a holy place made with human
hands, which was only a copy of the true one in heaven. He
entered into heaven itself to appear now before God on our

*behalf. And he did not enter heaven to offer himself again and again, like the high priest here on earth who enters the Most Holy Place year after year with the blood of an animal. If that had been necessary, Christ would have had to die again and again, ever since the world began. But now, **once for all time**, he has appeared at the end of the age **to remove sin** by his own death as a sacrifice.*[2]

176 Half of the Kingdom

I have been reflecting on the fact that two unsaved kings in the Bible each offered a half of their kingdoms to a woman. Esther, who became a queen, was one of them.

*And the king said to her, "What do you wish, Queen Esther? What is your request? It shall be given to you–up to **half the kingdom**!* [1]

The King offered Esther half of his kingdom one more time.

*At the banquet of wine the king said to Esther, "What is your petition? It shall be granted you. What is your request, up to **half the kingdom**? It shall be done!"*[2]

He even offered it to her a third time! The other woman was Herodias, daughter of Salome, who danced for King Herod and his guests.

*And when Herodias' daughter herself came in and danced, and pleased Herod and those who sat with him, the king said to the girl, "Ask me whatever you want, and I will give it to you." He also swore to her, "Whatever you ask me, I will give you, up to **half my kingdom**.*[3]

So, Father God, I am Your child, not a stranger, and I am asking You for half of Your Kingdom so that more souls will come into Your Kingdom! Amen!

177 The Language of Love

When children begin talking it is always the language of the person who raised them, usually their parents. How strange for English-speaking parents to raise a child, that from an early age, begins speaking a language unknown to the parents! Absurd!

God is Father to us all and His **language is love**. How ridiculous it is that God's children don't speak His language of love!

Help us Father, to speak Your language.

*A **new** commandment I give to you, that you love one another; as I have loved you, that you also love one another. By this all will know that you are My disciples, if you have love for one another.*[1]

The word '**new**' in "a **new** commandment I give you" doesn't mean 'brand new' but 'refreshed, as freshness'. This same command was already given to the Jews in the Book of Leviticus.

*You shall not take vengeance, nor bear any grudge against the children of your people, but **you shall love your neighbour as yourself:** I am the LORD.*[2]

Jesus was giving them a short refresher course on a word that they already had.

178 Two Realms

On my way to the city I was stopped at a red light and observed the traffic going by. Then the Holy Spirit had me ask myself this question:

"How many people that are going by are living only on the earthly realm of life?"

Of course, expecting an answer was not the point of the question. Rather, it was cause for deeper reflection and greater intercession for those who still are blinded by the ruler of this world, Satan.

We who have been saved by the Blood of Jesus Christ, are called to live here on earth in a very practical and useful way

Occupy till I come. [1]

Simultaneously, we are called to live in a realm that is higher.

*But God, who is rich in mercy, because of His great love with which He loved us, even when we were dead in trespasses, made us alive together with Christ (by grace you have been saved), and raised us up together, and **made us sit together in the heavenly places in Christ Jesus**.* [2]

*If then you were raised with Christ, seek those **things which are above**, where Christ is, sitting at the right hand of God. **Set your mind on things above**, not on things on the earth. For you died, and your life is hidden with Christ in God.* [3]

In what has been commonly called, 'The Lord's Prayer' or 'The Our Father' we read,

Your kingdom come! Your will be done on earth as it is in heaven. [4]

Again I mention, I love the way I once heard it: "As it is in heaven: yes, on earth."

How can we ever make His Kingdom come to earth if we only live in the earth realm? He has made it, not only possible, but it is His great passion and desire that would answer His call to come up higher and live in the heavenly realm too.

There are **two realms** and they are both for us now. Eventually, we will live a different life in heaven with heavenly bodies, but now we need to live in our 'earth-suits' and do heaven's business here!

179 Einstein's Mind

A few days ago, the Holy Spirit gave me the following analogy.

If I were a student of physics and someone told me, "You are now receiving **Einstein's mind**", I would go into my studies with wonderful confidence and my exams would be crowned with subsequent great success.

Yet God's Word, the Bible, declares that I *"have the mind of Christ."* [1]

Lord Jesus, even though I am writing it, and even though I believe it, I realize that there are whole levels of understanding and revelation that yet need to accompany this verse in my own life!

"I have the very mind of Christ." Christ, the Messiah, the King of the universe, the Maker and Creator of all that exists! Remarkable!

Lord, give me wonderful confidence and extra-ordinary success to accomplish all that You have called me to do. In this I trust that I shall prosper.

180 Xulon

After I had chosen **Xulon** (pronounced, zoo-lon) Press as a publisher for this book, I inquired as to what the word meant. To my great delight I found out that it is a Greek word meaning the tree of life.

The tree of life has been something I have reflected on for several years now.

The tree of life is first mentioned in the Garden of Eden in the Book of Genesis, and it is mentioned three times. [1]

Adam and Eve had to banished from eating from the tree of life or else they would have lived on earth forever in their fallen state. As it was, Adam lived 930 years, so strong was the life force that came from eating from that tree. Even his descendants, up till the time of the Flood, all lived remarkably long lives because of the life that was still in Adam's seed. There is an amazing chart depicting this in *The Living Torah*. [2]

The tree of life is spoken of three times in the Book of Revelation! [3] It is mentioned three times at the beginning and three times at the end of the Bible. It would appear to me that the tree of life is a type of book-ends for our lives.

There is a rabbinic saying: "The last thing to be done is the first thing that was thought of." For example, if you are building a house, when it is finished, that was the picture that you had in your mind at the beginning. What you get at the end, is what you thought of at the beginning. The completion of the thing makes the original thought obvious.

It would seem that from the beginning, God planned that we would eat from the tree of life. He has provided for us already through His Body and His Blood. [4] However, there is yet a greater future fulfillment of this word. More reflection!

Surprisingly though, the tree of life is also mentioned in the middle of the Bible, in the Book of Proverbs. King Solomon, in all his wisdom, wrote about the tree of life. [5] I see this as a major key: the fact that a very wise king included the tree of life in the Book of Proverbs and there it is mentioned four times. That makes a strong argument for its importance.

I desire all the life that is available to me, and it is available to me through Jesus Himself. He is the tree of life! Through Him I am satisfied! Through Jesus I have eternal life.

In the Book of John, Jesus declared that He was the **Bread of Life, the Resurrection and the Life, the Way, the Truth and the Life.** Why would I waste my time looking for life anywhere else? The Book of John speaks often about life. I encourage my readers to meditate on it for themselves: it is a well of living water.

Dear Jesus, You, are my tree of life. Thank You for revealing this to me. And now my prayer for all of the readers is that they will also find You, so that they too can have eternal life. May this book be a gift of life to all who read it! I ask this of You for Your honour and glory. Amen

181 Special Thanks

Give credit where credit is due!

I want to thank the Jewish people, more correctly, the Hebrew people, for the ultimate gifts of my life:

Thank you for **Yeshua** whose very name means **salvation!** This meaning is hidden to us in the English language but is very evident in Hebrew.

*Behold, an angel of the Lord appeared to him in a dream, saying, "Joseph, son of David, you must not be afraid to take to you Mary to yourself for your wife: for the One being formed in her is by the Holy Spirit. And she will give birth bring to a Son, and you will **call His name Jesus**, for **He will save** His people from their sins.[1]*

*And the angel said to her, Do not be afraid Miriam [Mary] for you have found favor with God. And behold, you will conceive in the womb and you will bear a son, and will **call his name Yeshua**. This One will be great, and will be called Son of the Most High; and the Lord God will give him the throne of David his father; and He will reign over the house of Jacob forever, and His kingdom will not end.[2]*

Yeshua is the only person on planet earth that chose His nationality and He chose to be a Hebrew: a Jew. He was from the tribe of Judah, a descendant of King David. He was born in Bethlehem; He ministered in Israeli towns and villages such as Nazareth, and Capernaum and in the region of the Galilee. He was crucified, died and rose again in the City of Jerusalem. Everything about *Yeshua* is very Jewish: very Israeli!

Thank you for **salvation**!

In the Book of John, we read the account of Jesus speaking to the Samaritan woman at Jacob's well. He made it very clear to her:

*We know who we worship: for **salvation is of the Jews**.*[3]

Thank you for the **Word of God**. It contains all the covenants and promises of God. Furthermore, through it I attain great peace.

... at that time, ye were without Christ [Messiah], being aliens to the commonwealth of Israel, and strangers from the covenants of promise, having n hope, and without God in the world.[4]

All the covenants and promises were given to Israel. As Gentile believers we have been wild olive branches grafted into the cultivated olive tree of Israel.

What would my life and my future be without these gifts from the Hebrew people?

Finally, because of all that I have received through the Hebrew people, I want to recount Paul's admonition to the believers in Rome.

*...I must go down to Jerusalem to take a gift to the Jewish Christians there. For you see, the Christians in Macedonia and Achaia have take up an offering for those in Jerusalem who are going through hard times. They were very glad to do this, for they feel that **they owe a real debt to the Jerusalem**

Christians. *Why? Because the news about Christ [Messiah] came to these Gentiles from the church [congregation] in Jerusalem. And since they received this wonderful spiritual gift of the Gospel from there, they feel that the least they can do in return is to give material aid.*[5]

I am a Gentile believer who has been blessed because of you. God's words to Abraham are being fulfilled every day:

...and in you and in your seed will all the families of the earth be blessed.[6]

Thank you very much Hebrew people! *Todah rabah!*

REFERENCES

Introduction
1-Psalm 149: 3 LB
1 The Purple Skirt
1-Philippians 4: 8 KJV
2 Microphone to the Universe
1-Hebrews 11: 1 LB
2-Isaiah 55: 11 LB
3 From a Teaching on the Radio
1-Matthew 13: 44 LB
2-Psalm 139: 13- 18 LB
4 pH Level 8
1-Matthew 5: 13 KJV
5 The Word is a Sword
1-Joyner Rick, *The Final Quest*, Morning Star Publications, PO Box 369, Pineville, N.C. 28134, Whitaker House, New Kensington, PA 15068, 1996
6 Jesus our 'Burden-Bearer
1- Isaiah 53: 3- 6
7 Cleansing Water
1- John 7: 38 LB
11 Enlarge My Tent
1-Isaiah 54: 2
2-Matthew 5: 43- 44... 46
12 God My Provider
1-Psalm 16: 5 LB

13 Conduits of His Presence
1-John 7: 38 LB
14 Entire Galaxies
1-Transcribed from a teaching by Rick Joyner in 1996.
2- 1 John 4: 4 KJV
15 An Ocean of Gratitude
1-Psalm 50: 14
2-This list is taken from Derek Prince's book, *Bought With Blood,* Published by Chosen Books, Grand Rapids, Michigan, 2000, 2007, by Derek Prince Ministries.
3-Psalm 128: 2- 4 LB
4-Philippians 4: 7
16 It Was Worth It
1-Hebrews 12: 2
17 Intergalactic Dancing
1-Esther 1: 6 LB
2-Psalm 11: 4 KJV
3-Psalm 115: 16 KJV
4-Job 38: 7 KJV
19 Feeling the Anointing
1-Verdusco Kovacs Ph. D. Amiee, *Dancing in the Anointing,* Treasure House Books, Destiny Image Publishers, Inc. P.O.Box 310 Shippensburg, PA 17257- 0310, 1996
20 I Am My Beloved's and My Beloved is Mine
1-Song of Songs 6: 3 ONM
2-Korson (Dorflinger), Esther,on line book: *I Am My Beloved's,* available free of charge
24 Water on a Duck's Back
1-Webster, *Webster's Dictionary and Thesaurus,* New Lanark, Scotland, 1990, Published by Geddes and Grosset Ltd, Windsor Court, New York, U.S.A
2- Isaiah 10: 27 KJV
25 Racing on the Runway or Lift-Off?
1-Romans 8: 6 LB
2-Exodus 19: 4 KJV
26 Money to Give Away
1-Matthew 6: 33 KJV

27 The X-wing Fighter
1- Isaiah 40: 31
28 Thank You for the Hard Times
1-Cahn, Jonathan, *Sapphires*, available for any donation from 'Hope of the World', Box 1111, Lodi, NJ 07644
29 The Dignified Bride
1-Revelation 19:7- 8 KJV
30 Luminescent
1-Hebrews 1: 14 KJV
2-Numbers 6: 24- 26 KJV
31 Suntan or Son-tan?
1- Psalm 116: 7
32 Guarding our Boundaries
1-Pierce, Chuck and Wagner Sytsema, *Riding Your Home of Spiritual Darkness,* Published by Wagner Institute for Practical Ministry, P.O. Box 62958, Colorado Springs, CO80962-2958, 1999
2-On the Northeast corner:
3-Psalm 91 10- 11
4-Revelations 2: 17
5-On the Northwest corner:
6-Psalm 91: 2
7-Revelation 3: 21
8-On the Southwest corner:
9-Psalm 91: 14- 16
10-Revelation 3: 12
11-On the Southeast corner:
12-Psalm 91: 1- 3
13-Revelation 2: 7
14-Psalm 147: 13
33 Cancer Healed
1- Isaiah 54: 17
35 The Sea of Galilee
1-Matthew 5: 44- 45
36 A Poem to the King
1-Psalm 45: 1 LB
2-Psalm 45: 1 Darby Translation

37 Teflon
1-Ephesians 4: 1- 3
38 One New Man
1- Ephesians 2: 12- 15 KJV
39 From Sumac to Oak Tree
1-Isaiah 61:3 KJV
41 God's Presence
1-John 14: 21 Darby Translation
43 Canada, Israel and the Bridge in Between
1-Psalm 2: 8
44 Prepare the Way
1-Song of Songs 8: 5
45 Healthy Body–Healthy Bride
1-James 1: 2- 4
47 Role Models
1-Isaiah 49: 6 LB
48 Joy from the Past
1-Philippians 1: 3- 4
49 Plugged In at New Levels
1-Ephesians 4: 15- 16
51 My Fair Lady
1-Romans 3: 23 KJV
2-Ephesians 5: 25- 27
3-Isaiah 61: 10 ONM
4-Ephesians 6: 10- 11, 14- 17
5-Colossians 4: 6
6-Psalm 19: 14
7-Song of Songs 1: 2 ONM
8-Song of Songs 2: 8-10
9-Matthew 11:28- 30
10 Corinthians 3: 1852
52 The Resurrection of the Dead
1-Taken from Jonathan Cahn' s *Sapphires*, July 31st 2013
53 The Lamp (The Menorah)
1-Matthew 5: 14- 16
54 His Magnificent Name
1-John 14: 13- 14

2-Song of Songs 1: 3
3-Philippians 2: 9- 11
55 Orchestrated in Heaven
1-Psalm 98: 1 ONM
59 Caterpillars and Butterflies
1-2 Corinthians 3: 18
60 Under our Feet
1-Romans 16: 20
61 Rain On the Just
1-Matthew 5: 45
62 A Cloud of Angels and Glory
1-Genesis 28: 11 ONM
63 Sun Screen
1-Psalm 121: 6
64 Trail Blazer
1-John 14: 6
2-1 Corinthians 3: 6- 9
65 The Ark of the Covenant
1-Numbers 6: 24 LB
66 The Storms of Life
1-Acts 27: 9-10, 15, 18- 19, 21- 26, 31, 33- 35, 42- 44
67 God and Money
1- Matthew 6: 24
70 Messenger of the Invisible God
1- Romans 10: 14- 15
71 A Polished Arrow
1-Hebrews 12: 7- 11 LB
72 How Odd of God
1-Wm. Norman Ewer 1885- 1976 Wikipedia: he was a British journalist
2-Cecil Browne, mentioned in conjunction with Wm. Norman Ewer[Wikipedia]
73 The Lord's Broken Heart for His People
1-Ezekiel 36: 21-23, 32- 33, 35- 37
2-Exodus 15: 11KJV
77 Better Each Time Around
1-Luke 12: 2

79 When I am Weak, Then I am Strong
1-2 Corinthians 12: 9- 10
2-Ephesians 6: 12

80 Prelude to Heaven's Fragrances
1-Song of Songs 4: 12- 13

83 Trying to Prove Who We Already Are
1-Matthew 4: 6 ONM
Matthew 3: 17 ONM
2-Genesis 3: 5
3-Genesis 1: 27 KJV

84 Praying for God
1-Joyner, Rick, *The Call*, Morning Star Publications, Charlotte, NC 28277- 2061, 1999

85 Magnify and Exalt
1-Psalm 34: 3

86 Thick Black ropes or Fishing Line?
1-Matthew 21: 31 ONM

87 The Power of our Words
1-Isaiah 53: 5 KJV
2-See # 58

88 Canadia?
1-Psalm 117: 1 KJV

89 Fresh Fruit
1-Galatians 5: 22- 23 ONM

90 Buying a Lie?
1-John 8: 31- 32

93 Spiritual Lessons from the Computer
1-John 14: 15- 17

94 Glorious Beauty
1-Psalm 30: 5 LB

96 Psalm 104: 30

97 The Greatest Talent
1-Matthew 25: 21 KJV

98 The Pain of Ingratitude
1-John 3: 16

99 Surrender!
1-*'Heneini'* is Hebrew for "here I am."..Taken from Isaiah 6:8

101 At Home With the Lord
1- 2 Corinthians 5: 6 LB
102 He is My Defense
1-Psalm 62: 6 ONM
103 Christ- Messiah
1-Copeland, Kenneth, *Pursuit of His Presence*, 1998 Kenneth Copeland Publications, Fort Worth Texas, 76192-0001, the reading for January 29th
104 So I Need You
1-Roundtree, Anna, *The Heavens Were Opened,* Published by Charisma House, part of Strang Communications Company, 600 Rinehart Road, Lake Mary, Florida, 32746, 1999
105 Hearing God's Voice
1-John 10: 27- 28
108 A Voice-Activated Kingdom
1-Psalm 27: 7
110 The Good Eye
1- Matthew 6: 22- 23 ONM
2-Luke 11: 34 KJV
3-Luke 11: 34 MSG
4-Proverbs 22: 9
111 Forerunner for a Special Season
1-Zechariah 14: 16 ONM
112 Pay Day for Jesus
1-Acts 20: 28
113 Wise Men Worship
1-Matthew 2: 2 **KJV**
114 Three Archangels
1-Roundtree, Anna, *The Priestly Bride,* Published by Charisma House, a part of Strang Communications Company, 600 Rinehart Road, Lake Mary Florida, 32747, 2001
2-Strong, James, *The Exhaustive Concordance of The Bible*, Abingdon Nashville, 1890
115 A Parable: The Piano Player
1-Psalm 16: 11
116 Our God is a Consuming Fire
1-Hebrews 12: 28- 29 KJV

117 Another Name
    1-Ruth 1: 15- 17
    2-Ruth: 2: 11- 12
    3-Matthew 1: 5- 6
118True Air Pollution
    1-Matthew 12: 34
    2-James 3: 2, 5- 6, 8- 10
    3- Psalm 19:14
    4-John 8: 26
    5-Proverbs 18: 21 KJV
    6-Proverbs 15: 4 KJV
    7-Matthew 12: 36-37
119 Great Men and Women of God
    1-Hebrews 7: 10
121 Illumination by Way of a Dream
    1-Isaiah 60: 1
122 More of You in My Life
    1-Psalm 27: 4
123 The Bread of Life
    1-John 6: 48- 51
    2-Genesis 3: 24
    3-Genesis 3: 22
    4-Mat. 26: 26
124 The Work of the Accuser
    1-Revelation 12: 9- 11 KJV
125 Prayers and Incense
    1-Revelation 5: 8
    2-Revelation 8: 3- 4
127 How Old Am I Really?
    1-Jeremiah 1: 5
    2-Ephesians 1: 4
128 Chosen and Faithful
    1-Revelation 17: 14 KJV
130 Parable of the Walnut Trees
    1-Psalm 92: 13 ONM
131 An Unlikely Place
    1-Exodus 5:1 KJV

2-Isaiah 55: 7KJV

138 For the Joy That Was Set Before Him
1-Hebrews 12: 2
2-Isaiah 53: 10- 12
3-Ellis J. Crum

139 My Holy Mountain
1-Psalm 48:1-2
2-Isaiah 11:9 KJV
3-Isaiah 56:7 KJV
4-Isaiah 57:13
5-Ezekiel 20:40
6-Daniel 9:16
7-Joel 2:1 KJV
8-Zechariah 8:3 KJV

141 How to Spell Israel
1-Deuteronomy 30: 5

142 Prayer in the Parking Lot
1-Isaiah 54: 1

143 Song: "O Israel"
1-Gambriel, Constance, Song: *O Israel*, Copyright 2001

144 Follower of Christ/Messiah
1-1 Corinthians 4: 16- 17

145 The Lands of Zebulun and Napthali
1-Matthew 4:15- 16
2-Judges 5: 14 KJV
3-Genesis 49: 21 KJV

147 Prophetic Gestures
1-Isaiah 33: 24 ONM

148 Jesus, the Lamb of God
1-Romans 8: 2 KJV

150 Beauty for Ashes
1-Isaiah 61: 3

152 Now I Know Why
1-Mark 11: 23- 24

155 God's Pity on our Clocks
1-Revelation 13: 18 NLT
2-Psalm 84: 11 KJV

3-John 1: 16 KJV
156 'Spider Man Like Activity'
1-John 14: 13- 14
158 Aaron's Staff
1-Numbers 17: 8
2-Romans 8: 2 KJV
159 A Prayer for Trust in God's Provision
1-Psalm 138: 8 KJV
160 The Price of Gas
1-Matthew 6: 33 KJV
161 Covenants
1-Psalm 89: 3 KJV
162 A Trauma Unit
1-Hebrews 13: 5- 6
163 Make your Breathing Count
1-Psalm 150: 6 KJV
164 Making Sweet Music
1-Cooke, Graham, *A Divine Confrontation*, Destiny Image Publishers, Inc. P.O. Box 310, Shippensburg, PA 17257-0310, 1999
2-Webster, *Webster's Dictionary and Thesaurus,*. New Lanark, Scotland, 1990, Published by Geddes and Grosset Ltd, Windsor Court, New York, U.S.A
3-Psalm 149: 1 KJV
165 Parable of the Filling Station
1-Psalm 27: 4- 5
166 A Vision of Sifting
1-Matthew 25: 31- 34
167 God's Son
1-Psalm 84: 11KJV
2-Revelation 1: 16 Darby Translation
168 The Cherubim and Seraphim
1-Genesis 3: 24
2-Hebrews 9: 3- 5
3-Isaiah 6: 1- 3
4-Hebrews 12: 29
169 Arise, Shine

1-Isaiah 60: 1- 2
170 Declaration Fulfilled
1-Johnson, Bill, *When Heaven Invades Earth*, Treasure House, Destiny Image Publishers, Inc. Shippensburg, PA, 2003
2-Mark 11: 23
171 Huge DNA
1-2 Timothy 2: 1- 2
172 Possess Your Possessions
1-Obadiah verse 17
2-Psalm 16: 5 KJV
3-Psalm 127: 3 KJV
4-Proverbs 11: 30
5- Psalm 1: 1- 3
6-Jeremiah 29: 11 LB
7-Exodus 15: 26
8-Isaiah 33: 24 KJV
9-Isaiah 53: 5
10-Jeremiah 30: 17
11-Acts 10: 38
12-Psalm 92: 12- 14
13-2 Corinthians 1: 20
173 Enough Jurisdiction
1-1 Peter 2: 9 NLT
2-Proverbs 10: 22
174 Keys of the Kingdom
1-Matthew 16: 19 NLT
2-Deuteronomy 30: 3- 4
3-Isaiah 43: 5- 6
4-Jeremiah 23: 3
5-Ezekiel 39: 25, 28
6-Zephaniah 3: 20
7-Zechariah 8: 7-8
175 Sources of Production
1-Romans 8: 1- 2 KJV
2-Hebrews 9: 24- 26 NLT
176 Half of the Kingdom
1-Esther 5: 3

2-Esther 5: 6
3-Mark 6: 22- 23
177 The Language of Love
1-John 13: 34- 35
2-Leviticus 19: 18
178 Two Realms
1-Luke 19: 13 KJV
2-Ephesians 2: 4- 6
3-Colossians 3: 1- 3
4-Matthew 6: 10
179 Einstein's Mind
1 Corinthians 2: 16 KJV
180 Xulon
1-Genesis 2: 9, 3: 22 and 3: 24
2-Revelation 2: 7, 22: 2, and 22: 14
3-Kaplan, Rabbi Aryeh, *The Living Torah,* Maznaim Publishing Corporation, 4304 12th Avenue, Brooklyn, New York 11219, 1982
4-See # 123
5-Proverbs 3: 18, 11: 30, 13: 12 and 15: 4
181 Special Thanks
1-Matthew 1: 20- 21 ONM
2-Luke 1: 30- 33 ONM
3-John 4: 22 KJV
4-Psalm 119: 165 KJV
5-Romans 15: 25- 29
6-Genesis 28: 14 KJV
Appendix # 1 – Salvation
Appendix # 2 – Romans 11:11- 29 KJV
Appendix # 3 – Recommended Reading

APPENDIX #1
SALVATION

Dear Reader,

After reading *Intergalactic Dancing*, you may want a personal relationship with Jesus and you're not sure how to go about it.

Jesus is the Son of God, who came to earth, took on a human form, lived in Israel 2,000 years ago and came to show us the way to His Father. He suffered at the hands of sinful men and was crucified and died on a cross. His Blood was poured out as a sacrifice for the sins of the whole world. You can read about His life in the Bible.

Because God is holy, no sin can enter heaven. We owe a debt for our sins that we can never pay, and so Jesus came and paid it for us through His Blood. We are all born with a sin nature and in need of forgiveness. The Bible says that we have all fallen short of God's glory. So we can never be good enough to get to heaven and we certainly cannot earn our way there, again that is why Jesus had to pay the price. Spiritually, we are all drowning and we need someone to save us: we have a Saviour and His name is Jesus!

You may be morally good, kind, helpful, generous, and very nice, but sin is still not forgiven. **All must repent**, that is, be willing to turn away from our sins and invite Jesus to forgive us. It is simply a matter of humbling ourselves and receiving what He has already provided for us. Besides, we were created for this spiritual connection.

It is quite simple:

1. **Admit** that you are a sinner, and be willing to turn from your sins with His help.
2. **Believe** that Jesus is the Son of God, who He died for our sins, that He rose from the dead, and that His Blood paid our debt in full.
3. Through **prayer and repentance**, invite Jesus to come in and take over your life through His Holy Spirit, that is, make Jesus the Lord and Saviour of your life. Remember, there is no sin too great that He isn't willing to forgive. He desires that no one should perish.

Prayer:
Dear Lord Jesus,

I believe that you died on the cross for me, and rose again from the dead. I know that I am a sinner in need of forgiveness. Please forgive me. Cleanse me with Your blood. I turn from my sin, with Your help, and I turn to You. I invite you to come into my heart and be my Saviour, and the Lord of my life. Holy Spirit, help me and strengthen me in the decision that I have just made. Amen.

Congratulations! You have just made the best decision of your life. Now, ask the Holy Spirit to help you find a Christian congregation that teaches the Bible. Purchase a Bible for yourself and read it every day. Go in His peace because Jesus lives within you by His Spirit.

APPENDIX # 2
ROMANS 11:11-29

M y reason for including these passages is that I have never
yet heard them preached in any church service outside of
Messianic gatherings or in Israel. Further meditation on Romans
11 will help us to understand our position regarding Israel, and
enhance our vision of God's purposes for His people.

*I say then, have they stumbled that they [the Jews] should
fall? Certainly not! But through their fall, to provoke them to
jealousy, salvation has come to the Gentiles. Now if their fall
is riches for the world, and their failure riches for the Gentiles,
how much more their fullness!*

*For I speak to you Gentiles; inasmuch as I am an apostle to
the Gentiles, I magnify my ministry, if by any means I may
provoke to jealousy those who are my flesh and save some
of them. For if their being cast away is the reconciling of the
world, what will their acceptance be but life from the dead?*

*For if the first fruit is holy, the lump is also holy; and if the root
is holy, so are the branches. And if some of the branches were
broken off, and you, being a wild olive tree, were grafted in
among them, and with them became a partaker of the root and
fatness of the olive tree, do not boast against the branches.*

But if you do boast, remember that you do not support the root, but the root supports you.

You will say then, "Branches were broken off that I might be grafted in." Well said. Because of unbelief they were broken off, and you stand by faith. Do not be haughty, but fear. For if God did not spare the natural branches, He may not spare you either. Therefore consider the goodness and severity of God: on those who fell, severity; but toward you, goodness, if you continue in His goodness. Otherwise you also will be cut off. And they also, if they do not continue in unbelief, will be grafted in, for God is able to graft them in again. For if you were cut out of the olive tree which is wild by nature, and were grafted contrary to nature into a cultivated olive tree, how much more will these, who are natural branches, be grafted into their own olive tree?

For I do not desire, brethren, that you should be ignorant of this mystery, lest you should be wise in your own opinion, that blindness in part has happened to Israel until the fullness of the Gentiles has come in. And so all Israel will be saved, as it is written:

The Deliverer will come out of Zion,

And He will turn away ungodliness from Jacob; for this is My covenant with them, when I take away their sins.

Concerning the gospel they are enemies for your sake, but concerning the election they are beloved for the sake of the fathers. For the gifts and the calling of God are irrevocable.

Let us be grateful for Israel. Let us pray for her and remember that we, as Gentile believers, are the wild olive branches grafted into the natural tree of Israel!

Appendix # 3
Recommended Reading

Archibold, Norma, *The Mountains of Israel- the Bible and the West Bank*, A Phoebe's Song Publication, 1993

Brown, Michael, L., *Our Hands are Stained with Blood*, Destiny Image Publishers, Shippensburg PA, 1992

Brown, Dr. Michael, L. *The Real Kosher Jesus*, Published by FrontLine, Charisma Media, Lake Mary Florida, 2012

Cahn, Jonathan, *Sapphires*, available at "Hope of the World", Box 1111 Lodi, N.J., 07644

Cahn, Jonathan, *The Harbinger*, published by FrontLine, Charisma Media, Lake Mary Florida, 32746, 2011

Cantor, Ron, *Identity Theft*, Destiny Image Publishers, Inc. Shippensburg, PA, 2013

DC Talk and Voice of the Martyrs, *Jesus Freaks*, Albury Publishing, Tulsa OK, 1999

Einspruch, Henry and Marie, *The Ox. . . The Ass. . . The Oyster...,* The Lewis and Harriet Lederer Foundation, Baltimore Maryland, 1975

Einspruch, Dr. Henry, *Raisins and Almonds*, The Lewis and Harriet Lederer Foundation, Baltimore Maryland, 1967

Ranklin, Judy and Davis, Ellyn, *The Physics of Heaven*, Double Portion Publishing, Crossville, TN, 2012

Johnson, Bill, *When Heaven Invades Earth*, Treasure House, Destiny Image Publishers, Inc. Shippensburg, PA, 2003

Johnson, Bill, *Dreaming with God*, Destiny Image Publishers, Inc. Shippensburg, PA, 2006

Johnson, Nita, *Prepare for the Winds of Change II*, Eagles' Nest Publishing, Omaha Nebraska, 1991

Joyner, Rick, *The Final Quest*, Morning Star Publications, Pineville, NC 28134, 1996

Joyner, Rick, *The Call*, Morning Star Publications, Charlotte, NC 28277- 2061, 1999

Koenig, Bill, *Eye to Eye- Facing the Consequences of Dividing Israel*, Published by About Him, Alexandria, Virginia, 2004

Kryskow, Faytene, C., *Stand On Guard*, Credo Publishing, Vancouver B. C., 2005

Lake, John G., *John G. Lake: His Life, His Sermons, His Boldness of Faith*, Kenneth Copeland Publications, 1994

McTernan, John and Koenig, Bill, *Israel the Blessing or the Curse?* Hearthstone Publishing, Oklahoma City OK, 2001

McTernan, John P, *As America has Done to Israel*, www.xulon-press.com, 2006

Morris, Robert, *The Power of Your Words*, Published by Regal Books, Ventura California, U.S.A., 2006

Prince, Derek, *Bought With Blood*, Published by Chosen Books, Grand Rapids, Michigan, 2000, 2007, by Derek Prince Ministries

Roth, Sid, *They Thought for Themselves*, Destiny Image Publishers, Inc, Shippensburg, PA, 2009

Roundtree, Anna, *The Heavens Were Opened*, Published by Charisma House, 1999

Roundtree, Anna, *The Priestly Bride*, Published by Charisma House, 2001

Saint. John, Robert, *Tongue of the Prophet*, Melvin Powers Willshire Book Company, Hollywood CA, 1952

Sheets, Dutch, *Authority in Prayer*, Bethany House Publisher, Minneapolis, Minnesota, 2006

Silk, Danny, *Culture of Honor*, Destiny image Publishers Inc. Shippensburg, PA, 2009

Stern, David H, *The Jewish New Testament*, Jewish New Testament Publications, Jerusalem Israel, 1989

Stern, David H, *The Jewish New Testament Commentary*, Jewish New Testament Publications, Jerusalem Israel, 1992

Wurbrand, Pastor Richard, *Tortured for Christ*, Living Sacrifice Book Company, P.O. Box 2273 Battlesville, OK 74005- 2273, 1967

Young Sarah, *Jesus Calling*, Thomas Nelson Publisher, Nashville Tennessee, 2004

BOOKLETS

Marcellino, Jerry with Yohanan Ben Yehuda, *Should Christians Have a Heart for Israel? A Biblical Perspective*, Published by Heart for Israel, Hartsville TN, 1960

Marcellino, Jerry with Yohanan Ben Yehuda, *Should the Nations Have a Heart for Israel? An Eternal Perspective*, Published by Heart for Israel, Hartsville TN, 1960

Marcellino, Jerry with Yohanan Ben Yehuda, *Should the Church Have a Heart for Israel? A Historical Perspective,* Published by Heart for Israel, Hartsville TN, 1960

CPSIA information can be obtained at www.ICGtesting.com
Printed in the USA
BVOW01s1943200114

342483BV00007B/22/P